Enhancing Brain Development in Infants and Young Children

Enhancing Brain Development in Infants and Young Children

Strategies for
Caregivers and Educators

DORIS BERGEN
LENA LEE
CYNTHIA DiCARLO
GAIL BURNETT

Foreword by Sandra J. Stone

TEACHERS COLLEGE PRESS

TEACHERS COLLEGE | COLUMBIA UNIVERSITY
NEW YORK AND LONDON

Published by Teachers College Press,® 1234 Amsterdam Avenue, New York, NY 10027

Library of Congress Cataloging-in-Publication Data

Names: Bergen, Doris, author. | Lee, Lena, author. | DiCarlo, Cynthia,
    author. | Burnett, Gail (Music teacher), author.
Title: Enhancing brain development in infants and young children :
    strategies for caregivers and educators / Doris Bergen, Lena Lee,
    Cynthia DiCarlo, Gail Burnett.
Description: New York, NY : Teachers College Press, 2020. | Includes
    bibliographical references and index.
Identifiers: LCCN 2020023701 (print) | LCCN 2020023702 (ebook) | ISBN
    9780807764442 (paperback) | ISBN 9780807764459 (hardcover) | ISBN
    9780807779125 (ebook)
Subjects: LCSH: Brain--Growth. | Developmental neurobiology. | Cognitive
    neuroscience. | Child development.
Classification: LCC QP376 .B487 2020 (print) | LCC QP376 (ebook) | DDC
    612.8/2—dc23
LC record available at https://lccn.loc.gov/2020023701
LC ebook record available at https://lccn.loc.gov/2020023702

ISBN 978-0-8077-6444-2 (paper)
ISBN 978-0-8077-6445-9 (hardcover)
ISBN 978-0-8077-7912-5 (ebook)

Printed on acid-free paper
Manufactured in the United States of America

Contents

Foreword

In our current quest to "educate" children, we often unwittingly neglect or diminish the *important things* needed for children to flourish now and into their future adulthood. Unintentionally, for example, a pursuit for "school success" can divert our attention away from the critical components of healthy brain development for young children to thrive as *human beings*.

Recently, I had a conversation with a parent who was more concerned about her 4-year-old's ability to memorize and trace letters than her child's play interests. The caring parent, of course, wanted the best for her child; this translated into preparing her child to be successful in school by practicing letters.

However, she did not have an understanding of the importance of play for her child's brain development. The parent did not know that playing prepared her child's brain for more important skills, such as the foundational ability to symbolize and think, that simply tracing letters could not provide. She did not know that play and experiences would give her child the necessary dynamic functions and neural networks for supporting future academics. She simply did not know how a young child's brain works and grows, nor did she know *how* she could support that important development.

This example illustrates how essential *Enhancing Brain Development in Infants and Young Children* is for today's educators, caregivers, and parents. Even though adults in the lives of young children should provide nurturing, rich, safe, and engaging environments for children to grow holistically, often adults are influenced by society to prepare children for school success instead of the best ways to promote children's optimal, healthy development. However, a narrow, one-size-fits-all curriculum view, with the expectations of compliance over ingenuity and production over process, often ignores children's innate curiosity, imagination, creativity, passion, and enormous diverse potential—and, of course, their holistic brain development.

Wisely, and with years of experience in understanding children and their development, the authors inspire readers to see children as developing *human beings*. With an unequivocal commitment to the well-being of children, they embrace the humanity and wholeness of each child. They do not accept the limited nature of learning, where children are accommodating robots or mimicking parrots. The authors prioritize children as being able to *think*, not replicate. They understand how *thinking* unfolds and have created an outstanding guide for the healthy and optimal brain development of young children. The authors open the door for understanding how the young brain develops, giving caregivers, educators, and parents an informative, practical guide to nurture this important development. For our caring parent, this book would give her confidence in supporting her own child's brain development by offering knowledge and guidance of how to provide appropriate play and experiences for her child.

In recent years, interest in brain development has led to significant research into how young children develop. Brain research is like a journey to an undiscovered world; it is captivating, intriguing, and exciting. But as interesting as this journey is, it is the *mission* that takes priority for the authors. The mission is to understand how this information will impact the lives of our young children; how we, as adults, can use the information to help and guide children. The authors have skillfully created a rich blend of research and practice to provide the important guidance adults need to accomplish this mission, contextualizing brain development into children's *human* experience.

In pursuit of these goals, the authors first support soon-to-be parents and parents of young children in their understanding of prenatal brain development and young children's developmental milestones. Second, the authors encourage caregivers and educators by providing case studies, thoughtful questions, concrete, real-life examples, and detailed, specific ideas for engaging children in music, art, science, social studies, social skills, and appropriate technology, offering opportunities and understanding for a wide variety of developmental domains for children from infancy through the early years to age 8. The ideas are definitely not a one-size-fits-all approach, but are designed to be appropriate for each child's unique, developing brain.

The ideas support empowering children's agency, giving them a sense of competency as active and effective learners and doers. The book guides adults on how to support autonomous children in following their own interests with choices of toys, materials, and experiences as they become independent, confident human beings.

The authors not only support brain development, but also appreciate the holistic nature of the developing child—cognitively, socially, physically, as well as regarding language and moral development. They address specific trends in young children's brain development with an understanding for individual differences, so adults can help with each child's unique brain development as their own distinctive timetable unfolds. The ideas presented by the authors are also inclusive for children with special needs.

In conclusion, I am greatly impressed by the authors' respect for children and their development, and the wise guidance they give the adults in children's lives. For example, they advise adults not to get caught up in just the care routines for children, but to focus on their vital role in providing a nurturing, engaging, interesting environment for our amazing children as they develop rich neuronal connections, and to guard against experiences harmful to their brain development. Equally, the authors' respect for our dedicated caregivers, educators, and parents who provide wonderful environments for our children is exemplary. This book will serve as a daily resource for early childhood advocates.

Enhancing Brain Development in Infants and Young Children stands out as a significant and inspiring contribution to the field of early childhood: a must-read for parents-to-be, parents, caregivers, and early childhood educators. This book addresses the *important things*—the remarkable attributes of brain development—but more importantly guides the reader to create environments and experiences for young children that will effectively enhance their developing brains, supporting children to flourish as human beings.

Our children, as *human beings,* deserve the best we can provide for them. Humanity demands our best for our children's present and future well-being.

Sandra J. Stone
Professor Emeritus
Northern Arizona University

Introduction

The authors of *Enhancing Brain Development in Infants and Young Children: Strategies for Caregivers and Educators* come from a variety of disciplines (early childhood education, early intervention, music education, and educational psychology) and philosophic orientations (Piaget, Bruner, Skinner, Montessori, Reggio Emilia, existentialism, and postmodernism) bringing unique perspectives and experiences.

Doris Bergen. When I was teaching preschool many years ago, Jean Piaget's studies of young children's thinking processes were being discussed widely in the United States, and I, as well as many other early childhood teachers, were made more aware of how young children try to understand their experiences. His work helped us observe the cognitive processes of children with whom we were working and consciously examine how children's thinking seemed to differ from that of adults. Many early childhood teachers began to realize how important their work is in promoting brain development.

Later, as a university teacher of early childhood education courses, I was influenced by another set of researchers and authors who wrote about specific ways the human brain develops both prenatally and over the first 7 years of life and about how poverty, institutionalization, and aggressive conditions can be harmful during these important brain development years. From my own observations, I had noticed how young children's experiences are quickly reflected in their behavior and realized how important positive and rich experiences are for their brain development and for their cognitive, social, emotional, physical, language, and moral development. Thus I believe there is a strong case for helping parents and early childhood educators provide great "brain growth" environments for young children.

Lena Lee. As an early childhood teacher educator, researcher, former teacher of young children, as well as a mother, I have always been interested in brain development. How the human brain works fascinates me and I often apply what I know about brain development when I teach students, as I raise my own child, or even as I motivate myself. Recently, I have witnessed that American children suffer from mental illness and emotional instability more than ever before and in greater numbers. In addition, students come from many different socioeconomic and cultural backgrounds in American society. As a result, I have looked for ways to support all these children effectively by implementing a variety of approaches in early childhood classrooms.

It is well known that a child's first 5 years are critical for brain development. However, I have noticed that there are not many professionals, parents, and policymakers who know what to do with this information. I believe it is important for early childhood educators and parents to know how young children's brains develop, how positively or negatively they change depending on environmental factors, and how we can provide brain-positive ways to improve young children's meaningful experiences. This knowledge can offer every child opportunities to learn in better, as well as more socially just, ways. This book is for those who teach, interact with, and educate young children and who want not only to know more about brain development of young children, but also how to take a "brain-friendly" educational approach.

Cynthia DiCarlo. I began my career in the field as an early interventionist in the public school system, working in a self-contained classroom of preschoolers with a variety of disabilities.

Although grounded in developmentally appropriate practices literature, I incorporated the behaviorist paradigm in practice to help young children with special needs learn essential skills. Upon transitioning to a birth-to-3-year-old inclusive program, I also implemented a more embedded style of behavioral intervention within the context of the early childhood classroom.

My work has been influenced by Bandura's social learning theory and Vygotsky's sociocultural theory, embracing the role relationships play in learning. Brain research suggests that stress negatively impacts learning, attention, and problem solving. For children to learn optimally, they need strong relationships with caring, supportive adults. After many years in the classroom, I transitioned to the university, where my research focuses on interventions to improve outcomes for young children and clarification and innovations in recommended early childhood practices. My classroom teaching experiences have had a great impact on my university teaching, as I retained a practical orientation to theory and its implementation in the classroom.

Gail Burnett. I have been a lifelong musician, but I learned about the important links between music and brain development initially through my work with the Music Together® program, for which I taught and directed a Music Together Center for 15 years. The work and research of Music Together's Kenneth K. Guilmartin and Lili M. Levinowitz in the areas of early childhood music research focus on how children develop musically, and this view has been instrumental in my teaching, songwriting, and teacher training sessions.

That, in conjunction with my hands-on "real-life" experience working with and performing for children, has given me the foundation to expand work in the areas of music and movement for children aged 0–6 and to write and incorporate music that is developmentally appropriate, brain enhancing, and inclusive of children with special needs. I also have a passion for creating and training teachers about how to incorporate a musical environment in the classroom that can foster an emotionally safe and cohesive environment for children, especially for those who may not have an emotionally safe environment at home.

PURPOSE OF THIS BOOK

We have designed this book to explain clearly to early childhood caregivers and educators what is presently known about prenatal and early childhood brain development, to help them be aware of the important role their childcare and teaching practices can play in facilitating positive brain development, and to give them practical suggestions for brain-enhancing curricular practices for these crucial developmental years.

Most abilities human beings need throughout their lives are connected to their early brain development; thus the strength and vitality of these early brain-expanding processes will affect children's behaviors for the rest of their lives. Early caregivers and educators already provide many of these "brain-enhancing" experiences, but they may not have specific knowledge about how their practices are related to children's brain development or how to explain these developmental processes to parents. The purpose of this book is to make them aware of these relationships and help them know how to speak with parents about these issues.

OVERVIEW OF THE BOOK

Chapter 1 gives basic information on brain development during prenatal, infant, toddler, and early childhood years. It also includes definitions and diagrams that give students basic background information about the brain and its processes. For each age level there are case examples, including a focus on prenatal practices that may harm fetal brain development.

The next four chapters relate the knowledge presented in Chapter 1 to early childhood teaching practices that can positively affect brain development. Each chapter reviews details of brain development at one age level: infancy (Chapter 2), toddlerhood (Chapter 3), preschool (Chapter 4), and kindergarten/early grades (Chapter 5). These chapters also describe how practical educational strategies and curricular ideas may be related to brain development at that particular age level. Ideas include ones related to musical and artistic expression, active physical play, language, math, science, and social–emotional behaviors. Each chapter also includes ideas for enhancing brain development for children with special needs and suggests ways to educate parents about brain development at that age level.

The final two chapters discuss the roles of technology and broader societal influences that educators must understand. Chapter 6 gives early childhood teachers practical strategies and curriculum ideas related to the use of various technological devices and explains how these are related to child brain development at the focused ages. It includes ideas for teachers and for parent education. Chapter 7 discusses other contemporary issues that may be affecting the brain development of young children, both potentially positively and negatively. It also notes long-range societal issues that may affect young children's brain development and encourages advocacy on the part of early childhood educators for improving societal practices that can enhance brain development of all young children.

ACKNOWLEDGMENTS

The authors thank the many children, parents, students, and teachers with whom we have worked over the years for giving us the experiences that inform the content of this book. We welcome the opportunity to share our knowledge and curriculum ideas and hope that readers will find them useful as they strive to promote the healthy brain development and meaningful education of the children in their lives.

The Brain Building Process

During the past 20 years, researchers have learned much more about brain development before birth and during the first years of life. They now stress how important the prenatal environment and young children's early experiences (birth to age 8) are in supporting optimum brain development. Although some brain development continues throughout life, this earliest time period is when most "brain building" occurs.

Educators are becoming aware of the special opportunities they have in influencing children's brain development by promoting activities that increase the richness of young children's brain communication pathways, the density of their vital nervous system connections, and the complexity of their brain's cerebral patterns. Teachers need to share this information with parents to help them provide early experiences that foster their children's brain development during these important years. This chapter gives an overview of the processes of early brain development and explains both

Figure 1.1. Brain Diagram

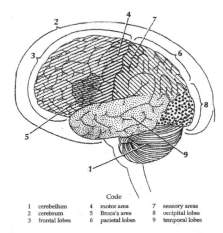

Code

1	cerebellum	4	motor area	7	sensory areas
2	cerebrum	5	Broca's area	8	occipital lobes
3	frontal lobes	6	parietal lobes	9	temporal lobes

Diagram from Brain Basics, *published by the National Institute of Neurological Disorders and Stroke.*

Source: Brain Basics, Know Your Brain. Published by the National Institute of Neurological Disorders and Stroke https://www.ninds.nih.gov/).

the roles of family members and early childhood professionals in fostering children's good brain development. Figure 1.1 shows the major areas of the brain when it is fully developed.

PRENATAL BRAIN DEVELOPMENT

Susie's Pregnancy and Care

Although Susie, aged 17, suspected she was pregnant, she tried to ignore the possibility for as long as she could because she really did not want to have a baby. When she finally realized she could not pretend that this pregnancy was not happening, she asked her best friend, Judi, to go with her to a clinic in her neighborhood. After her examination, Susie was told that the fetus was already about 4 months along. She agreed to try to change her lifestyle when the physician told her that drinking alcohol and taking various other drugs would be harmful for the infant's development. Susie is going to find this very hard to do, however, since that is the lifestyle that her group of friends really enjoy (including Brad, the likely father of the baby). The clinic staff encouraged her to join a "motherhood" group of young pregnant women to make some new friends. Susie doesn't live with her parents, so she has decided to wait to tell them about the pregnancy; she is undecided about telling Brad.

Many people, including many pregnant women, do not realize how important the 9 months before birth are for an infant's brain development. However, the prenatal period is when the essential elements of the brain are constructed. Over half of all human genes are involved in brain development, and during pregnancy these genes are active in building the basic brain structures, as well as in creating the initial parts of the neuronal network, which will be greatly expanded after birth (Siegel, 2015). Infant brain development begins at one end of the *neural tube*, the initial fetal form that develops into a baby. The neurons that make up the brain begin to develop early, and it is during the 12–20-week fetal period (about the first 3–5 months) that almost all of the neurons that a person will need throughout life are generated (Corn & Bishop, 2010). Also during this time period, the basic sections of the brain are built.

The brain areas that develop earliest are the ones that support basic motor and sensory activity, as well as abilities such as balance, vision, hearing, taste, touch, and pain sensitivity. When the fetus is about 3–5 months old (the midgestation period) the process of building the higher cortical centers of the brain begins (Bielas, Higginbotham, Koizumi, Tanaka, & Gleeson, 2004). This process involves the "traveling" of neurons up "cortical ladders" made of glial cells to gradually build the cortex area of the brain. From about 25 to 30 weeks is the most critical time for development of the auditory system and, in contrast to the visual system, the fetal hearing system needs auditory stimulation to develop (Graven & Browne, 2008).

In the cortex, the language areas in the left side of the brain grow larger and the fetal brain even starts to respond to different types of language sounds. Research has shown that infants who have been exposed to music during the prenatal period begin to hear and respond to musical sounds from about 19 weeks gestation (Hepper & Shahidullah, 1994). Other important areas that develop during the later months of prenatal development are the memory areas of the brain, as well as other sections involved in higher thinking processes. Figure 1.2 provides a description of major brain areas and the processes associated with them.

Because prenatal brain building activity is so important and will have lasting consequences for the person's lifelong development, every pregnant woman should try to exercise good care for herself during pregnancy. She should avoid substances such as nicotine, alcohol, and opioids because these can harm the fetal brain building process. Also, the pregnant mother should receive good nutritional care because the fetal brain needs quality nutrition. Extreme malnourishment can permanently harm fetal brain development. Pregnant women should have previously received inoculations for common diseases. Illnesses such as measles, as well as other less common ones (e.g., the disease caused by the Zika virus), can negatively affect the fetal brain building process (Adibi, Marques, Cartus, & Beigi, 2016; Chua, Prat, Nuebling, Wood, & Moussy, 2017).

Figure 1.2. Areas of the Brain and Associated Processes

Amygdala: part of the inner brain (temporal lobe) involved with experiencing emotions

Basal ganglia: cerebral structures involved in controlling motor movements

Cerebellum: part of the hindbrain, involved in motor coordination, learning, and memory

Cerebrum: rounded outer brain structure divided into two hemispheres

Cortex: outer layer of the brain

Cortical migration: the prenatal process in which neurons travel from lower brain areas to form the cortex

Forebrain: section that includes the cerebral hemispheres, thalamus, and hypothalamus

Frontal lobe: part behind the forehead, concerned with behavior, learning, personality, and voluntary movement

Glial Cells: the most abundant cell type in the central nervous system, which surround the neurons and both support and insulate them

Hindbrain: lower part of brainstem, including cerebellum, pons, and medulla oblongata

Limbic system: networks in the brain involving basic emotions (fear, pleasure, anger) and drives (hunger, sex, dominance, care of offspring)

Motor cortex: portion of the cortex that initiates and controls voluntary muscular activity

Myelination: the process that puts insulating sheaths on the axons of the nervous system

Neuron: the basic unit of the nervous system, including cell body, dendrites, and an axon, which processes and transmits information

Parietal lobes: the brain area at top of head, concerned with sensory information

Pruning: the process that controls eliminating synapses

Temporal lobes: the sides of the brain where speech and language regions are located

Visual cortex: the occipital lobe section of the cerebral cortex, which processes visual information

---

The cortical structures and other parts of the brain may not be built correctly if any of the following occur during pregnancy: illness, fetal exposure to drugs or alcohol, and poor nutrition (see Agrawal et al., 2010; Honein et al., 2001). Any or all of these negative issues can result in brain building problems. It is very important for educators who work with pregnant women to make them aware of how important the care they give themselves during pregnancy is in fostering the brain growth and health of their infant.

If all goes well during the pregnancy period, at birth infants will have about 100 billion neurons in their brains (Bergen & Woodin, 2017). These are the neurons the person will use throughout life. However, many of these neurons are not yet connected in communication networks; thus they are not yet good communicators of complex messages. During the infant to preschool years one of the major tasks of the brain is to build functioning brain communication networks. Thus the richness of experiences that young children have determines how well their brains will expand these communication networks and enable them to function as a thinker and a doer throughout life. Because most of the building of the brain's communication networks happens in early childhood, the role of early caregivers and educators is vitally important. These people in the child's life can help them build their excellent brains.

INFANT BRAIN DEVELOPMENT

The Noah Family and Their Premature Infant Drew

Although Lala was very conscientious in following all the diet and other care advice during her pregnancy, she began having contractions in the 7th month. Her doctor advised that she take leave from her job and have bed rest so that the infant would not arrive prematurely. Lala followed her doctor's advice, but even so, baby Drew was born 5 weeks prematurely. At birth, he weighed less than 4 pounds, his extremities were bluish, and he had trouble breathing. Drew was diagnosed with Respiratory Distress Syndrome (RDS) and placed in an incubator to receive supplemental oxygen therapy. Lala spent part of each day at the hospital and Lee, her partner, visited every evening, but they continued to worry until at last the baby was deemed of sufficient weight (5½ pounds) to be discharged. Because Drew was so small and had started his life precariously, both of his parents were nervous and anxious, especially when he did not seem to be doing well at nursing and his sleep patterns were erratic. However, now that Drew is 2 months old, they are beginning to relax and are starting to enjoy their baby as he begins to be more easily cared for.

At a typical 9-month birth, infants already have many abilities because the neuronal communication areas of the brain that are essential to life (e.g., breathing, sucking, crying, and temperature regulation) are basically functioning. Also, the sensorimotor areas of the cortex, which control reflexive behaviors (e.g., rooting, sucking, stepping reflex, grasping, and startle), are already active. Young infants show physical responses, such as cooing, waving hands or feet, or moving eyes toward musical and other sounds (Hepper & Shahidullah, 1994). Because of their prenatal sound/music experiences, newborns are already sensitive to both the language and the music of their culture. Premature infants sometimes have difficulty with meeting basic survival activities because their brain is less developed, and they usually need special care until these brain areas have become more mature. The developmental pattern of premature infants will lag initially but usually by year 2 they are reaching typical growth markers.

A recent study found that premature infants' sensorimotor brain development benefits by having supportive and caring touch by caregivers (Maitre et al., 2017). By 2–3 months, the full-term infant's neuronal connections in parietal, temporal, and primary visual cortex areas develop further and promote the infant's sensory development. The neurons increase in size and become connected in more dendritic networks and these neural connections also begin to communicate faster due to the *myelination* (i.e., protective covering) of the glial cells that cover the networks. There also is the beginning of maturation of the basal ganglia and cerebellar hemispheres of the brain. See Figure 1.2 above for definitions of brain sections and functions.

Infant caregivers usually notice that infants gain many skills around 3 or 4 months, and this is due to a brain growth spurt at that age. According to Schore (2001), the infant's right hemisphere, which has deep connections to limbic and autonomic brain areas, has greater development during the infant years, and that hemisphere activity supports the development of infant attachment relationships to caregivers. The infant's responses to music and other sounds also becomes more refined and sustained. During this first year, infant nutrition is very important because it provides the energy infants need for their optimal brain development.

At about 6 months, the infant's higher brain centers (i.e., cortex areas) gain more connections, and by 8 months caregivers notice that the infant begins to understand many more things, due to increased activity in their frontal lobes. By about 9 months, infants have enough motor control to grab, manipulate, mouth, deliberately drop, and look for objects. Their play can involve interacting in "peekaboo" and other baby games with familiar caregivers. They begin to understand some words in their native language and express meaningful sounds, and by 1 year of age, they show that they know the sounds of their native language. Although infants can express emotion at an early age because the *amygdala*, a part of the limbic system or "old brain," is well formed at birth, they only begin to understand and label their emotions at about 1 year, when the limbic cortex begins to mature.

Infants' attachment to caregivers, often expressed in stranger anxiety in the latter part of the first year, is evidence that the medial frontal lobe of the brain is developing, and they are able to distinguish between familiar and unfamiliar people. Infants also start to both understand and imitate the actions of others as their "mirror neurons," located in the parietal and frontal lobe, begin to mature (Rizzolatti & Craighero, 2004). This development also can be seen in their intense interest in watching the facial expressions and the motor actions of both adults and other children (Coudé et al., 2016). Infants also begin to control their attention to such actions, especially if these activities are ones they enjoy.

Recent research in which brain activation of the prefrontal cortex was observed when adults and 9-month-old infants interacted in play showed that both infant and adult prefrontal cortex (PFC) channels and some parietal channels were intercorrelated, indicating that the neurons of both individuals were acting together (Piazza, Lasenfratz, Hasson, & Lew-Williams, 2020). Also, the brain prefrontal cortex was activated for both the infants and adults preceding moments of mutual gaze; this activation increased when the infant smiled. Infant brain activity was also related to changes in the pitch of the adult's speech. Such experiments confirm the importance of infants' early interactive experiences with other humans.

An environment that supports infant brain development, therefore, involves infants in developing sensorimotor skills related to seeing, listening, touching, moving, and babbling by providing opportunities for them to use their existing abilities to explore and learn about their environment and to respond to many caring and playful human interactions. Because the sensorimotor areas related to sound perception and music are active in infancy, they are very responsive to such stimuli. One study showed that infants who participated in interactive music classes with their parent or caregiver demonstrated earlier sensitivity to pitch structure and brain responses to music (Trainor, Marie, Gerry, Whiskin, & Unrau, 2012).

Other activities enjoyed by infants during this age period, such as being touched, reaching for and touching people and objects; looking, tasting, and manipulating objects; and being bounced, swung, or lifted are all evidence of the developmental changes in these various brain areas. The understanding that infants gain from their physical interactions with the environment is characterized as *enactive cognition*, which is gaining knowledge by touching, feeling, mouthing, holding, shaking, and engaging in many other physical behaviors with the objects and people in the environment (see Bruner, 1964). The neonatal brain weighs about 1 pound, but by the end of the first year, because there is so much growth in the brain's neuronal connections, the infant brain weighs about 2 pounds. Figure 1.3 shows how the neurons that are minimally connected at birth become richly connected by age 6 and less diversely connected by age 14, after pruning has occurred.

Figure 1.3. Changes in Synaptic Density from Birth to Adolescence

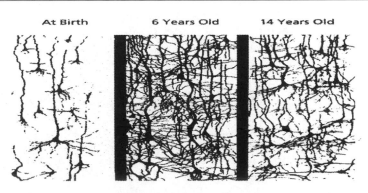

Note. Drawings by H. T. Chugani.

TODDLER BRAIN DEVELOPMENT

Amata's Activity Level

Amata's mom, Marta, is having a hard time getting used to the way her child's behavior has changed since she started to walk at 13 months. Now, at 15 months, Amata is into everything. She was a very easy baby who ate well without stomach upsets, learned to sleep through the night, and was responsive but not demanding of attention. After she learned to toddle around the furniture and examine many parts of her surroundings, her mother has realized that there are potentially dangerous places in her apartment. For example, Amata has picked up and tasted items that were dirty or might contain lead, and she has broken two of Marta's favorite dishes by banging and dropping them. Since Marta never learned much about child development, she is thinking that Amata is becoming a naughty child because she gets into everything and often uses her new word "no." Since they live on the third floor of an old building and the stairs leading to their place are dark and rickety, Amata must be carried up and down to go outside. There is a tiny yard, but the grass is sparse, and the street has a lot of traffic so there are not good outdoor places for Amata to play. Marta has been offered a part-time job, and she is now searching for an inexpensive day care that Amata can attend and "learn to behave better" while Marta is working.

The toddler years are a time when the brain's neural connections continue to be made at a very rapid pace. The growth of the brain's sensorimotor areas makes toddlers' sensory and motor control stronger and the brain's hemispheric growth enables toddlers' right- or left-handedness to be established. Thus they can do many more actions to affect their environment, like throw a ball, pat a toy bunny, or open the kitchen cupboard door. Also, brain development in the *parieto-temporal* areas, where perceptual and language skills are located, shows up in the toddler's perceptual and language growth spurts and they gain more ability to control their attention. Toddlerhood is a peak time for growth in language understanding and in speaking as the two major brain areas related to language (Broca's and Wernike's) have a major increase in synaptic connections. A vocabulary burst occurs at about 16–20 months and a later comprehension burst occurs at about 30 months. Usually by 18 months, toddlers can begin to talk about what they remember about events or objects, and this development is related to maturation of the memory areas in the brain.

Long-term memory is situated in the hippocampal area of the medial temporal lobe, but other memory storage areas are in the medial thalamus, basal forebrain, and prefrontal cortex. That is, memory processes are widely distributed in the brain. By age 3, basic cognitive abilities such as attention and memory are well established, and children at age 3 can use simple memory strategies such as repetition to remember something. Although toddlers' ability to understand and regulate emotions is not at adult level, the emotional centers in the lower limbic system begin to gain stronger connections with the frontal lobe (the *thinking* part) of the brain. Because they now have language, they can begin to tell how they are feeling ("mad," "sad").

Another very important developmental milestone occurring early in a toddler's 2nd year is pretending. Toddlers can begin to act *as if* they can drink pretend tea or talk to their "baby" doll. This ability to pretend will be greatly extended during the later preschool years, but the simple toddler pretend actions are crucial for supporting the further development of pretense. They also can imitate pretend actions that they have been shown by adults or other children. Toddlers still show much of their cognitive growth in enactive cognition, which involves touching, moving, and experimenting with real objects, but they also begin to show *iconic* cognition, as they start to label pictures of objects in books and name people in photographs. According to Bruner (1964), it is essential for humans to develop these types of cognition before they become able to understand symbolic thought (letters, numbers).

During toddlerhood the brain is developing so fast that adults often notice that toddlers seem to learn many new things every single day. That may be because their brains are two and a half times as active as adult brains. By the age of 2, the number of neuronal connections (*synapses*) in the toddler brain is about the same as the number in adult brains, and by age 3 the child's brain has about twice as many synaptic connections as the adult brain. The toddler brain also has more chemical communication facilitators (neurotransmitters) and a higher metabolic rate. Increases in brain weight are also partly due to the increase in the speed of message transmission, which is facilitated by the increase in myelination, a process that covers neuronal connections with a substance that increases communication speed. Because of these increases, brain weight at age 3 is about 3 pounds.

Toddlers seem to be learning all the time, and sometimes they may learn many things that adults wish they did not learn. Their imitative skills and their activity level may result in their trying to engage in actions that adults do not yet think they are competent to do, such as wash dishes or turn on the television. It is common for toddlers to begin to assert their own ideas and desires, and sometimes these conflict with those of adult caregivers. Adults should recognize that toddler assertion of their own ideas is evidence of their brain development and should give them opportunities to make choices of activities.

An environment that supports toddler brain development, therefore, involves putting toddlers in safe but appropriately challenging environments in which they can actively engage in exploring their many developing skills. Their experiences (primarily playful ones) should be accompanied by rich

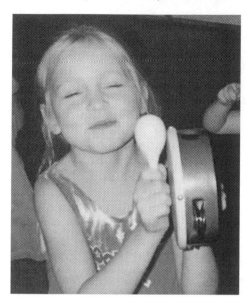

and varied language environments, encouragement of mastery of both small and large motor skills, and opportunities to engage in social interactions with other children and with caring adults.

PRESCHOOL BRAIN DEVELOPMENT

The Mumbara Family

The Mumbara family has been in the United States for only 8 months; during this time, with the help of their sponsors, they managed to find housing and part-time jobs for both parents. They don't work at the same time, so one of the parents is always caring for their 3½-year-old son, Sumi. Recently they were surprised to get information about their child being eligible to enter a Head Start program offered in the small city in which they live. The parents both went to a meeting (bringing Sumi with them) to learn more about this program, and they were encouraged to sign up their child for the 4-mornings-a-week class that would be starting the next month. Since they had never heard of this program, they were hesitant about sending their child because he is still so young and they were not sure that he would be happy away from his parents. However, they decided to let him attend. With the help of the Head Start staff, they were able to complete the information necessary to enroll Sumi. When they took their child to his Head Start class for the first time, they were amazed at the furniture, toys, and other materials in the room. They also were pleased that their child seemed comfortable in this new environment.

Now that Sumi has been going to the morning program for a few weeks, they are already seeing a different child. Before attending, Sumi had been shy and quiet, but now he is speaking up at home, is active in his play, and does not like to be babied. The parents are beginning to wonder if they made the right decision sending him to Head Start because such behaviors are not always appreciated in their culture. They are uneasy about their involvement because the teachers are expecting them to participate more in Sumi's activities at home.

The preschool age period is an especially important time for the rapid growth of the brain's communication systems. *Synaptogenesis*, which is the development of new synapses that connect the neurons with each other, continues rapidly and the brain is especially active making these connections during this period. In fact, by age 4 the brain is so active that the cerebral metabolic rates of glucose utilization are two times normal adult levels. Myelination (covering the neuron networks with an insulation sheath) of brain networks also continues and this makes flow of information faster. As myelination occurs in the limbic system, the child's speed of communication connections is greatly increased.

As different brain areas mature, there also are changes in the amount of blood flowing in the brain. At about age 3, the sensorimotor areas and the parieto-temporal areas have high blood flow, indicating refinements taking place in fine-motor, sensory, gross-motor, and language regions, and signaling changes in motor, sensory, and language skills. The 3–6 age period also is the time of the fastest growth rates in the frontal lobe areas that regulate the ability to plan new actions. As the frontal lobe continues to mature, preschoolers begin to have *source* memory, which is awareness of where and when something was learned. Sometimes they remember things that parents would prefer they forgot.

Teachers and parents can observe preschool children's social development, language growth, and increases in symbolic representation in their interactions and play with peers, especially in their advanced levels of pretend play. Elaborate pretense involving other children and long-term pretend themes that go on for many days is a major type of play at this age level, as children continue to expand their ability to act "as if." Researchers have found that preschool children's brain development and thinking is both similar to and different from that of older individuals. In one study of 4–6-year-old children's brain waves, measured as the children tried to reason about reality and false-belief questions, researchers found that there were differences in the left scalp brain waves between children who failed or passed false-belief questions (Liu, Sabbagh, Gehring, & Wellman, 2009).

Other studies have looked at the effects of direct teaching on preschoolers' brain development and found that various types of training can affect the children's attentional networks. In one music training study, the preschoolers who received music training were found to be better at show-ing auditory selective attention, which is being able to focus on specific sources of sounds or speech (Neville et al., 2008). Because preschool chil-dren's brain development is especially strong in the cortex (the higher brain centers) there is an increase in cortical volume, in gray and white matter tissue growth, and increasing metabolic demands. However, young children still need to have a greater number of brain regions active to complete de-manding cognitive tasks.

Researchers (e.g., Brown & Jernigan, 2012) recommend that more study of preschoolers' brain development should be done because of the great importance of these years, which show such dynamic and robust brain growth. They know that if children have high growth and expansion of synaptic connections during these preschool years, then more dense and extensive brain resources will be available to them when the later brain pruning becomes active.

Because the preschool age period is such an important one for brain development, an environment that supports this development is especially important. Preschoolers should be involved in interesting and challenging environments that allow them to expand their experiential base. Expe-riences that stimulate all brain areas include physical activity, social in-teraction, cognitive challenge, and emotional strengthening. Varied and interesting engagement with other children as well as with adults should enable them to learn many ways to master challenges. These experiences should be accompanied by rich and varied language opportunities, en-gagement in social interactions, and appropriate opportunities to master many social, physical, and cognitive skills.

Also, during this age period children's brains make quick connections not only for body coordination but also for cognitive skills, language ac-quisition, and emotional development. Because their brain development is quite fast and intense, preschool-age children want to try many new and varied things. They use trial-and-error experimentation to learn how things work—which adults often see as mischievous behavior and getting into trouble. When they play, they focus more on what and how they play (i.e., the process) than on what they have at the end of play (i.e., the product). Thus deciding on how to play and what to play are more important for them than gaining a product as a result of play. This explains why they might build a house with blocks for hours and then run into that house to break it in a second. While some aspects of preschool brain development may make preschoolers' behaviors more challenging for adults to under-stand and appreciate (e.g., wanting to choose for themselves what to do and what to wear; asking questions that adults may not want to answer), this is evidence that they are increasing their lifelong brain capabilities.

It is typical during this age period that cultural differences show up in the behavior expectations of adults toward their children, especially

regarding the behaviors expected of male and female children. For example, parents from diverse cultures may have different learning or developmental areas that they think are important (Ojala, 2000) or have styles of parenting that are more permissive or demanding of child performance (Domènech Rodriguez, Donovick, & Crowley, 2009; Varela et al., 2004). Presently, however, it is unclear whether the variance in expectations make permanent differences in brain development, and this question is only beginning to be a topic of study (see Ambady & Bharucha, 2009).

KINDERGARTEN/PRIMARY YEARS BRAIN DEVELOPMENT

Janie's 2nd-Grade Year

Janie started 2nd grade with great enthusiasm, as she has always been an eager learner and interested in many things. Her kindergarten and 1st-grade teachers were both advocates of active learning, and so they had many different activities and projects that engaged Janie deeply. They dealt with her rather short attention span by including a variety of ways to learn the same concepts, and there were opportunities for her to make choices about the ways she would learn academic skills. During the summer before she started 2nd grade, her parents noticed that she no longer was as interested in activities that involved physically challenging skills. She started to focus her interests on drawing and writing books and making elaborate small worlds with her blocks, small dolls, and other miniature toys, and she usually chose the same two playmates, both girls who were a year older. In 2nd grade, Janie seems to put less effort into her learning at school. She complains to her parents that the teacher makes everyone do the same thing and practice math and reading concepts over and over, even if these tasks are ones she already knows how to do. Her parents plan to talk to the teacher about how to help Janie regain her enthusiasm for learning while also meeting the demands of the 2nd-grade curriculum. They are wondering if she could work on special projects when she has finished her routine work or whether she could test out of doing some of that work.

Although synaptogenesis (creation of neural networks) continues to occur throughout the period of ages 6–8, this also begins a time when the process of *pruning* (i.e., cutting back on) neural networks becomes more prominent. At about age 7, the synaptic density of the frontal lobe of the brain is at its highest and children are developing greater motor coordination, metalinguistic awareness, self-efficacy knowledge, and social competence. Some researchers (e.g., Bauer, Lukowski, & Pathman, 2011) are studying potential differences that might occur in male and female brains (e.g., hippocampus larger in girls; amygdala larger in boys), but more research is needed to determine how such differences might be related to behavior differences.

During this age period, the amount of energy (as measured in glucose use) needed for the brain gradually declines as the pruning process occurs. However, children of this age continue to activate larger brain areas than adults when carrying out discrimination and other cognitive tasks. As the frontal lobe begins to mature, which improves cognitive and other abilities, some abilities seem to mature earlier than others do. For example, children's memory and problem-solving processes seem to advance in speed. By age 6, there are already individual differences in how children's brains have developed, with phonological awareness, vocabulary, and mathematical abilities showing some different patterns. There are gains in speed of reaction times and cognitive test performance during this age period.

One very interesting brain development is related to the appearance of the *P300 brain wave* (Sangal & Sangal, 1996), which is not present in younger children. The P300 brain wave is thought to be related to making humans conscious of their mental experiences, but it does not reach full amplitude and speed until adolescence. Typically, during thinking processes children activate many neurons initially and, in order to think clearly, they may have to ignore some unnecessarily activated neurons during a learning task. By age 6 or 7, however, children usually can focus more successfully on tasks requiring attention and, although it still takes greater effort than it would for adolescents or adults, they can inhibit impulses that encourage them to choose other behaviors. For example, by this age most children can forgo eating one marshmallow in order to wait to get two marshmallows (Mischel, 2015). This ability to focus on tasks assigned by others instead of on activities that are of interest to them is an essential skill for children's success in school-related learning.

As the neuronal networks begin to mature, children's processing speed also grows faster and children ages 6–7 can improve their performance on tasks requiring attention and inhibition of impulses. It appears that schooling itself improves memory skills as well as promoting general cognitive development, and formal learning environments may enable the brain's memory functions to operate more efficiently (see Vygotsky, 1978; Roberts et al., 2015). These changes in brain wave functioning are congruent with the time period that Piaget (1952) labeled *concrete operational thought*, in which children's thinking about concepts of number, space, weight, and volume becomes similar to adult thought. This is additional evidence that cortical growth cycles are concurrent with cognitive developmental cycles. These cycles of cognitive development follow a definite reorganizational pattern in the brain, which is evident primarily in the prefrontal cortex.

During this age period there are refinements and individualization of brain structures and functions, and, as children interact with environmental experiences, their interests may become more pronounced in new areas and less focused on activities they enjoyed at earlier ages. Studies of executive functioning at different age levels show that certain brain waves absent in younger subjects appear at this age level. For example, brain activation during children's performance on academic tasks show that beginning readers' brain patterns differ from those of both preschoolers and older readers (see Pugh et al., 2013).

Cognitive problems such as learning disabilities and attention deficit disorders, which may be related to issues of brain maturation, are often diagnosed in this early elementary time period. The kindergarten and early elementary years are particularly important for children who come from environments where positive and challenging early experiences are not necessarily promoted. Because their brains are still open to neuronal growth and the establishment of important cognitive connections, educators can greatly enhance these children's brain development.

Although the brain maturation process enables children to be more focused on adult-directed activities, an appropriate environment for kindergarten and early elementary students should continue to provide a wide variety of physical and sensory experiences and age-appropriate challenges that foster both cognitive and social understandings. Playful exploration of environments and creative opportunities that enable consolidation of learning skills and promote greater cognitive and social understandings are important at this age level. The richness of the learning environment is especially important for kindergarten/primary-age children because the more synaptic connections that are strengthened and diversified, the greater their physical, social, cognitive, and emotional abilities will be enriched and strengthened.

Children at this age level still enjoy long periods of play and can usually play well with their friends. They solve problems such as what shape Lego blocks are needed to build a strong castle and what they should say to friends and teachers when they want a specific material that other friends or the teachers may have. As a result, during their play children learn not only how to think creatively and differently about a situation or a problem, but they also learn how to communicate with, negotiate with, and understand the views and desires of other people, which helps them develop the concept of their own identity. Thus play helps children learn *who they are*.

BRAIN DEVELOPMENT ISSUES FOR CHILDREN WITH SPECIAL NEEDS

Arthur's Reading Difficulties

Although Arthur seemed to be typically developing throughout his preschool years, in 1st grade he began to be upset when it was time for his reading group because he did not want to be included in the slow group of children who were having difficulty learning to read. He managed to achieve the ability to read at 1st-grade level by the end of the year with a lot of practice and encouragement from his parents. When he was in 2nd grade, however, his teacher recommended that he have a comprehensive evaluation by the school psychologist. Although the evaluation showed that in many areas Arthur was above average cognitively, it also showed that he had weaknesses in phonological processing and reading fluency. Therefore, the psychologist recommended that he have special training to improve his phonological skills and increase reading fluency. With this extra assistance, Arthur was reading on grade level by the end of the school year.

Unfortunately, there are many young children who encounter learning difficulties that may be related to brain development, and these are often identified during the primary school age period. As is the case with Arthur, there may be no obvious underlying brain development issue identified in the first few years of life. Thus, the child develops typically or even exceptionally well in many areas before a learning disability can be identified during this age period. However, some disabilities are related to genetic abnormalities (e.g., Down syndrome), poor environmental conditions in the womb (e.g., nicotine, opioid exposure), or extremely bad care concerns in the child's early years of life (e.g., abuse, food deprivation, lack of human contact) (see Perry, 1996).

Being in deprived or stress-producing early environments can affect the brain's neuron development processes and immune systems and can affect young children's physical, cognitive, and social–emotional abilities. Brain scans of children who have experienced severe neglect show that the amygdala, which regulates emotions, is not the same size as the amygdala in the brains of young children who have not experienced neglect. Even when children are in growth conditions that are only *less* enriched than what is typical, their brains may develop differently. For example, research has shown different levels of vocabulary growth and types of words children speak depending upon how much their mothers talked with them (Hart & Risely, 1974, 1975). Because of the developmental harm that may be associated with relatively poor environments, it is very important that caregivers and educators provide both safe and appropriately challenging early childhood experiences when they have opportunities to work with such children.

Research also has shown that some genetically related brain problems may show brain development and behavior differences in the earliest years. For example, *autism spectrum disorder* (ASD), which has a wide range of severity, often is diagnosed during the 2½–3-year-old age period, when most children show a spurt in language and social skill development. These children may be averse to eye gaze or they may not engage in social or pretend play. *Down syndrome* is a chromosomal abnormality syndrome (an extra chromosome: trisomy 21) and usually is evident in child impairments in cognitive, linguistic, social, emotional, and motoric skills in the first few years of life. Children who have Down syndrome often have strengths in visual processing, receptive language, and social skills, and building on these strengths is very important. Thus it is essential for early childhood caregivers and educators to provide early intervention to help all of these young children develop optimally.

It is especially important for caregivers and educators to consider children's developmental age, not just chronological age, when working with those who have identified special needs. Caregivers and educators should have an extensive understanding of child development and brain development, using this knowledge to support children where they are, while providing adult support (e.g., verbal, gestural, or physical assistance) in working toward more advanced skills. Some children may need increased time to achieve a chronological milestone, while others might need a material modification (e.g., an adaptive spoon to eat, picture cards to make a choice) to successfully complete a task. Because optimum brain development from prenatal to early elementary years is crucial for children's lives, those who work with young children should be knowledgeable about ways they can help children develop their brain's optimum capabilities.

Another category of children with special needs are those who seem to develop brain-related abilities considered advanced for their age level. For example, they may be interested in learning all about specific subjects (e.g., trains, birds) at age 2, learn to read at age 3 or 4, or enjoy making up math problems at age 5. These are the children who are usually labeled "gifted." Often both parents and teachers of such children have difficulty allowing them or enabling them to learn and explore the world at the level that is appropriate for their brain development. Because these children's brains appear to be extremely active and possibly have much more synaptic development during the early childhood years, it is important for them to have encouragement and support for the activities and advanced learning they crave. They should not be required to relearn information they have already mastered if that is the level of the curriculum; rather they should be allowed to explore and investigate the knowledge and activities that their brain development level requires.

FOSTERING BRAIN DEVELOPMENT: ROLE OF FAMILY AND EARLY CHILDHOOD PROFESSIONALS

Brain development research has shown how important it is for family members and early childhood caregivers and educators to know how to help young children's brains develop well through the social, emotional, cognitive, physical, musical, and other learning experiences they provide. It is essential that pregnant women and their families know how important the fetal environment is for healthy brain development, and all family members need to be aware of the importance of the first years of life in promoting optimal brain development. Because many children are now cared for by grandparents and other relatives, it is important that those family members also understand the types of care and education experiences children need for healthy brain development.

Early childhood professionals can be influential in fostering children's brain development in many ways. First, they can play a role in informing pregnant women about good prenatal care and helping them to find providers of good care. Second, they can help educate family members on appropriate care and educational experiences for young children and regularly provide home learning experiences. Third, they can have a vital role in promoting brain development both in their own programs and in their family-related teaching. They can support the parents' role in their children's education through increasing awareness of developmental milestones and how to promote learning in the home. Examples of learning opportunities include incorporating developmental skills within routine tasks and activities (e.g., meal times, bath, storybook reading). This can be accomplished by capitalizing on their own child's interests by following the child's lead. Also, in the early childhood care and education programs they provide, educators can greatly support and ensure that children's experiences are ones that promote positive brain development.

SUMMARY

The first years of life mark a period of rapid brain development. Early childhood educators need to know about this important process of brain development across the early years, and how to support healthy brain development (e.g., supportive, nurturing adults; rich environments) and to guard against experiences that might harm brain development (e.g., stress, illness).

QUESTIONS FOR DISCUSSION

1. If you were aware of a pregnant woman who was smoking or drinking alcohol, how would you help her understand why she should stop those behaviors during the pregnancy?
2. What programs exist in your community to help educate parents on prenatal care and development? What resources might you direct families to?
3. In an infant care program, how important is it to provide sensory and physically active experiences for the children and how might such experiences affect brain development?
4. What suggestions might you give parents of toddlers to support their development in the home environment?
5. What are some suggestions for parents of preschoolers that would help them provide more opportunities for their children to use their increasing competence?
6. How can families support a kindergarten-age child's increasing cognitive, language, and mathematical competence?
7. How might knowing about the importance of good brain development for toddlers, preschoolers, and kindergarten/primary-age children affect the types of experiences educators might provide for typically developing children? For children with special needs?

SUGGESTIONS FOR FURTHER READING

Bergen, D., & Woodin, M. (2017). *Brain research and childhood education: Implications for educators, parents, and society.* New York, NY: Routledge.

Eliot, L. (1999). *What's going on in there: How the brain and mind develop in the first five years of life.* New York: Bantam Books.

CHAPTER 2

Fostering Brain Development in the Infant Curriculum

Min

When Min was born at 22 weeks gestation age, she had an extremely low birth weight and thus she spent 4 months in the neonatal intensive care unit. Although she has progressed well, she needs human contact to facilitate her language and problem-solving skills. At 10 months of age, Min is a spirited young girl, but she is functioning at the 6-month level and just beginning to scoot toward toys in the classroom. Due to delays in her development, she has been placed with children younger than her chronological age to correct for prematurity. She is increasingly curious and explores items using her hands and her mouth. Because she frequently cries when left unattended, her teachers have a variety of battery-operated cause/effect toys that they use to keep her entertained. When Min pushes a button, she is rewarded by several minutes of flashing lights and music. However, this slows down her exploration, as she is mesmerized by the lights and sound. While pushing a button requires motor movement on Min's part, the feedback she receives does not require much movement, and limits her motivation to move and explore other toys that may provide her opportunities to develop additional skills. Also, when she is engaged with the battery-operated cause/effect toys, she is interacting less with others in her environment and, when she is occupied with this activity, teachers are interacting with her less because she is seemingly occupied.

Daniel

At Daniel's 1-year-old birthday party, his parents planned music activities for the slightly older children who had been invited to the party. When he hears these music activities start, Daniel becomes wide-eyed and participates in typical 1-year-old infant fashion. For the "egg shaker song" he holds an egg in each hand and shakes the eggs intermittently as the music plays, but only occasionally is he "on the beat" with the music. He also explores the egg shakers in other ways: putting them in his mouth, throwing them, putting them down, crawling away, and picking them up again. When his mother holds him, she models the "beat" for him with the eggs she is holding. He watches her and the other children, but he does not follow any of the movement patterns. However, he seems joyful just holding the eggs and making his own movements. Similarly, when children wave the scarves to music, he waves his scarf randomly, but he squeals with joy when his mother plays "peekaboo" with the scarf. Daniel's mom also picks him up and "dances" to the music and he responds to the music through his mother. As she moves, he seems to sense himself as making the movement. While Daniel is not able to imitate specific music movements, he seems to enjoy music and having opportunities to imitate movements.

Lola

Since birth, Lola has not been an "easy" baby as she did not take well to breast feeding, slept for relatively short time periods during the night, and carefully observed her environment. She especially was interested in watching her older sibling, 3-year-old Sally, as she moved around the house engaging in activities. Now that Lola is 7 months old, she becomes fussy if she is kept in the crib or bounce chair very long. She is happiest on the floor, sitting, rolling around, and scooting (she is not yet crawling), picking up toys and other objects, shaking them, and putting them in her mouth. Her parents have recently noticed that she is already trying to pull herself up by grabbing at the low table. She is also starting to "talk," and some sounds she makes seem almost like words. Her parents are surprised that she is already "getting into everything" because Sally had been a very placid child who did not walk until she was over a year old. Lola seems to have a lot of muscle strength and a desire to get moving much earlier than Sally did, so her parents think she may start walking at an earlier age. They sometimes think her natural curiosity behaviors are her being "naughty" and they think about putting her in time-out when she gets into things. They are not sure that they are prepared for such an active child!

REVIEW OF BRAIN DEVELOPMENT AT THE INFANT AGE LEVEL

In planning infant curriculum, it is important to consider how infant brain development occurs during that first year. Figure 2.1 gives a review of brain development information at the infant age level.

Figure 2.1. Review of Brain Development at the Infant Age Level

- At birth, the areas of the brain that are essential to life are basically functioning, and sensorimotor areas of the cortex, which control reflexive behaviors, are already active.
- At birth, areas of the brain responsive to sound are also responsive to musical sounds, such as changes in tempo, volume, and melody changes, evident in infants' sensory and motor responses.
- By 2–3 months, the infant's neuronal connections in parietal, temporal, and primary visual cortex and motor areas are maturing.
- During the first 6 months, neurons increase in size, become connected in dendritic networks, and begin communicating faster due to myelination of the glial cells.
- At 3 or 4 months, maturation of the basal ganglia and cerebellar hemispheres occurs, and this brain growth spurt is evident in the growth of the infant's motor, social, perceptual, and cognitive skills.
- By 6 months, the infant's higher brain centers (i.e., cortex areas) gain more connections and become very responsive to physical and social interactions.
- By 8 months, there is increased activity in the infant brain's frontal lobes, and cognitive development is evident in the infant's actions on the physical objects in the environment.
- By 9 months, infants have motor control to grab, manipulate, mouth, deliberately drop, and look for objects, as well as motor skills to sit, crawl, pull to stand, and (for some) initiate walking.
- By 12 months, the infant brain is responsive to language, and infants can engage in social play that involves rudimentary pretense.
- Although the brain systems always operate as a whole, during the first few years of life some right-brain areas appear to mature slightly faster than some left-brain areas. Thus young children's response to social–emotional interactions may proceed slightly faster than their response to language and other cognitive skills that are primarily centered in left-brain areas.

Note: Premature infants' brain development milestones will occur on a later time schedule, but their development will still follow this order unless they have severe developmental problems.

FOSTERING BRAIN DEVELOPMENT AT THE INFANT AGE LEVEL

It is easy to forget that having a new person (an infant) in one's life involves major changes in all aspects of an adult's experience. At least for the immediate future, new parents must put aside their own desires and instead respond to the needs of this relatively helpless but already demanding person. For adults who have life problems or who are immature in their own development, this first year of their child's life may seem especially daunting. Yet, even for adults who eagerly awaited the birth of their child and had prepared carefully for meeting the infant's needs, the first year will have many challenges. Of course, there also will be many enjoyable aspects of caring for and engaging with the infant, especially in promoting early play and social interactions.

Knowledge about important brain development processes that go on during the first infant year can help families and other caregivers be more appreciative of how their efforts to care for, enhance, play with, and encourage their infant's brain development can make the task of infant care more satisfying. Thus the educational and support role of caregivers and educators is especially important for parents during this first year of the child's life.

Fortunately, even adults who are not especially knowledgeable about infant development can get correct messages about how best to meet infant developmental needs because infants are good at demonstrating these needs as the various areas of their brain's develop. If adults understand the processes of infant brain development, they can be aware of these processes and support the infant's changing needs, behaviors, and skills by adapting their behaviors to the new infant behaviors that are promoted by the infant's neuronal growth and maturation.

In contrast to commonly held opinions, those who care for infants play an especially important role in fostering early brain development. Infant caregivers must be aware of both typical and atypical brain and behavior milestones so that they can adapt their own behaviors to keep up with brain-related growth spurts, behavior changes, and developmental challenges that occur in rapid succession during the first year of an infant's life. Infant caregivers (i.e., educarers) must revise their interactive behaviors with infants as the infants indicate that they are becoming more capable and aware.

CURRICULUM PRIORITIES AT THE INFANT AGE LEVEL

Especially important for brain development during this age period are curriculum experiences that engage infants in the following activities:

1. Sound/music/pattern play
2. Responsive and warm adult facial expressions and talk during both caregiving activities and playtimes
3. Large, simple picture viewing and adult talk about pictures
4. Many safe opportunities for repetitive motor skill practice
5. Encouragement of simple object play with a range of safe materials
6. Environmentally clear but challenging mobility patterns and pathways
7. Initiation of rudimentary pretense interactions (i.e., pretend play) by adults

Many of these activities initially involve direct and responsive interaction with adult caregivers but, as infants increase in their abilities, they will initiate and expand on many of these activities themselves. Because infants' skills change often, their environmental experiences also should change frequently to meet their expanding skill development patterns. Educators should continually revise their interaction patterns and the environmental play opportunities to meet and challenge infants' developing abilities (see Bergen, Reid, & Torelli, 2009).

It is *definitely not recommended* to place infants in swings, jump chairs, or other automatic movement devices, nor is it ever recommended to place them in front of television or smartphone images. These "automatic stimulation" devices are tempting for infant caregivers to use, but they diminish the "human to human" and "object engagement" interactions that are vital for infant brain development. Although long-term effects of such practices on brain development are presently unknown, the time spent with such devices takes time away from the human and "real-world" environmental interactions that infants need to foster synaptic richness in their brains.

The following section suggests a sample of curriculum activities that may facilitate infant brain development. Of course, there are many other activities that also can be relevant for this development. The growth areas addressed below use the National Association for the Education of Young Children (NAEYC) standards labels.

SAMPLE CURRICULUM ACTIVITIES

Because infants change so much during the first year of life, some activities are suggested for ages 0–6 months and others for ages 7–12 months. At all ages and with any activity it is important to smile and keep eye contact with the infant whenever possible. Individual children may differ in their skill level so some crossover of the recommended appropriate activities is expected. The most important skill the adult can have is being able to note and respond to the developmental growth of the infant and to adjust curriculum activities appropriately. It also is important to provide information on developmental milestones/screening tools to inform parents/caregivers of emerging skills in infants. This also can help parents promote these skills at home and identify when/whether their infant may need early intervention services to support development.

Activities for Ages 0–6 Months

WHO DID THAT?

Domain: *Physical Development:* Repeats random movements; shakes rattle
Social/Emotional Development: Maintains eye contact; smiles
Language Development: Vocalizes in responses

Procedure: While the infant is on their back, place a wrist rattle or rattle sock on one leg. Gently bring the rattle into the infant's visual field and shake the rattle while making eye contact and displaying a surprised expression or vocalizing ("Wow!"). Wait for the infant to repeat the hand or leg movement, praising effort by providing eye contact, smiling, and displaying surprise in facial expression and vocalization. Rotate the wrist rattle or rattle sock to different arms/legs and repeat activity to encourage purposeful motor movement and increased coordination.

YOU DON'T SAY!

Domain: *Language Development:* Engages in vocal turn taking
Social/Emotional Development: Turn taking

Procedure: While in close proximity to the infant, listen to the sounds they make and repeat the vocalization. Pause to allow the infant to vocalize again. Each time they vocalize, the adult should repeat the vocalization. This is the beginning of conversational turn taking.

HERE YOU GO!

Domain: *Physical Development:* Shifting weight from side to side in a lying position; reach and grasp objects
Language Development: Engaging in vocal turn taking

Procedure: Place the infant on stomach and elbows. Get down on the floor with a few rattles. Shake a rattle and hold it out for the infant, using language to verbally encourage them to reach ("Here you go! Take the rattle!"). If necessary, help the infant shift their weight to one side in order to move arms forward or place a small rolled towel under arms as a bolster. To encourage crossing midline, place the toy on the side opposite from the infant's free hand, covering the other hand with yours if necessary. Generously praise. Give breaks as needed. Repeat with different rattles for as long as the infant remains interested.

Rhythmic Movement Play

Domain: *Physical Development:* Shift weight from side to side in a lying position; reach and grasp objects; body spatial movement
Creative Expression/Arts Appreciation: Respond to musical sounds and movements

Procedure: One important thing to know is that young infants perceive the adult's body as an extension of theirs. When you hold an infant and jump, dance, bounce with rhythm, and make other movements, the infants "feel" the beat as if it were in their own body. Thus an important musical activity to do with infants is to make large movements to music, including the following:

- Holding the infant securely in arms, swing them back and forth to the beat.
- Holding the infant securely, jump or bounce with them in your arms.
- Holding the infant securely, "dance" to the beat.
- The adult can also move an infant's feet and arms to the beat when the infant is lying down or help the child "bounce or jump" up and down to the beat of a song.

Singing

Domain: *Physical Development:* Fine motor/facial expressions
Language Development: Hearing language sounds; musical sound cognition
Creative Expression/Arts Appreciation: Responding to musical sounds/movements

Procedure: Singing to an infant is an important musical activity. With the infant lying down, in a sling, or being held, sing "face to face" so the child can see your facial moments as you sing. Exaggerating your mouth movement when you sing, having your eyes wide open, and smiling as you sing are all ways to engage the infant more effectively. You do not need to be an expert singer and you can sing whatever type of song you like, since it is the sound, rhythm, and facial movements to which the young infant will attend.

Just Do Like Me

Domain: *Physical Development:* Fine motor/eye coordination
              Language Development: Imitating verbal communication

Procedure: Initiate some movements and actions to see how infants can do the motions you do. You can clap, shake your head, pull your arms high, touch your nose or ears first and tell them to do the same. You should always verbally communicate with them as you do this because they will learn not only physical and eye coordination skills but also language skills from you! Also use simple percussion instruments like egg shakers, rattles, and drum rattles to do this.

Funny Faces

Domain: *Social/Emotional Development:* Imitation; interacting with
                  caregiver
              Physical Development: Fine motor/eye–hand coordination

Procedure: Make a facial expression you have seen the infant make before, such as opening their mouth, sticking out tongue, opening and closing eyes, or smiling. Perform the facial expression and see if the infant imitates you. When they do, provide positive feedback through verbal praise and smiles.

Modification: Imitate a facial expression the baby has just performed and see if they will repeat the facial expression again.

What Do You Want?

Domain: *Physical Development:* Reaching
              Language Development: Expressing a preference

Procedure: Take two toys and put them in front of the infant, presenting each in the middle of their eye gaze, then holding one in each hand horizontally to give the infant a choice of toys. Be sure the infant has made visual contact with each toy. Give the infant the toy that they reach for or that their eyes linger on after having visual contact with both toys.

Modification: Beginning at 4 months, you can encourage a reach by physically guiding the infant's hand to the toy that their eyes have lingered on. Note: If the infant reaches for both toys with both hands, hold the object vertically .

Who's That?

Domain: *Physical Development:* When on stomach, pushing up on elbows
Social/Emotional Development: Interaction with caregiver; looking at self in mirror

Procedure: Place infant on their stomach and place a nonbreakable mirror in front of them. Get on the floor and place your head over the mirror and encourage infant to look up at the baby in the mirror. Provide verbal praise and smiles to encourage them to raise their head to look at you and to see their reflection in the mirror.

Modification: You can use a rolled-up hand towel or bolster to put under the infant's arms to help them support their body. Note: Be attentive to signs of fatigue and move the infant to another position when they shows signs of fatigue.

Activities for Ages 7–12 Months (Can Be Adapted for Toddlers)

Object Play

Domain: *Social/Emotional Development:* Giving and receiving objects
Physical Development: Using wider arm movements; manipulating objects

Procedure: As infants gain motor and sensory skills, they learn by exploring familiar items. Clean and safe kitchen materials such as plastic containers, paper plates, small pans, big spoons, water bottles, plastic cups, and other items should be provided for exploratory play. These should be of various colors, weights, and sizes and made of materials that very young children can safely touch, shake, suck, and throw. By 6 months of age, infants enjoy putting these objects into other container-like objects and then dumping them out, and they will do this same activity over and over. By exploring features of many objects, infants gain knowledge of the objects in their world (i.e., enactive cognition).

Mirror Play

Domain: *Social/Emotional Development:* Recognizing self; interacting with adult
Physical Development: Using fine motor skills

Procedure: By about 6–9 months, infants who can sit or stand up can enjoy playing with a mirror. Securely attach a mirror on the classroom wall or, with an adult present, place it on the floor or the table. They can sit or stand in front of the mirror while you talk about their body parts such as eyes, nose, head, and hands. Initially, the infants will be able to point to the body part on their bodies, but generally they cannot point to that body part on their reflection in the mirror. Model to them by pointing to themselves in the mirror image and lead them to see their reflection. You also can show other actions and ask them to follow your actions. Clap once and ask them to clap; make a big smile for the happy face and ask them to smile like you; or make two hands raise just above your head like rabbit ears and ask them to do that. There are many body actions infants can imitate.

RHYTHMIC MOVEMENT PLAY

Domain: *Early Literacy/Early Mathematics:* Recognizing patterns
Social/Emotional Development: Interacting with adult
Physical Development: Using balance and gross/fine motor
  skills
Creative Expression/Arts Appreciation: Responding to musical rhythm and movement

Procedure: Caregivers can engage infants in rhythm play whenever music is present, even when an activity is not "intentional." For example, when infants can sit up, you can sit on the floor with legs stretched out, with the infant sitting on your legs and facing you. While you rhythmically bounce their knees gently up and down, the infant can "ride a horse." Making the "clip clop" sound with the tongue while bouncing on the same beat is not only fun for the infant but reinforces rhythm. Looking, smiling, and interacting gives the infant comfort and connection with the caregiver while making music. This allows them to both feel and "see" the hand movement, while hearing the rhythmic beat and their name.

MUSIC INSTRUMENT PLAY
(NOTE: ADULT PRESENCE/INVOLVEMENT AT ALL TIMES IS ESSENTIAL)

Domain: *Physical Development:* Using controlled arm movements;
  manipulating objects
Social/Emotional Development: Giving and receiving objects
Creative Expression/Arts Appreciation: Responding to musical rhythm and movement

Procedure: Child-safe instruments, such as egg shakers, drums, maracas, or bells, are fun for older infants to use. At this developmental stage, they will be exploring, very possibly putting the objects in their mouths, or playing with them instead of making any meaningful music gestures. The best way to engage infants is to allow them to explore the instrument while the adult models the rhythm, keeping a steady beat with their own instrument. Some infants will watch but not participate except to hold the instrument while others will begin to shake it (although not initially with the beat!). The caregiver can help infants understand this action by gently tapping or keeping a beat on the child's back, leg, or foot so they can "feel" the beat as well.

SCARF MUSIC PLAY

Domain:　　*Physical Development:* Using controlled arm movements; manipulating objects
Social/Emotional Development: Giving and receiving objects
Creative Expression/Arts Appreciation: Responding to musical rhythm and movement

Procedure: Using scarves with music can be very enjoyable for older infants. Multicolored sheer scarves are the best choice for this activity. You can make the scarves "dance" to the music for the infant when they are either in a sitting or lying down position. Also, you can "dance" holding the scarf and the infant. Infants also love to play "peekaboo" with the scarves. This can be done along with the beat of the music while the infant sits facing the adult. Or you can sing on a specific pitch: "peek-a-BOO!" At the infant stage, it is the act of surprise that is the most fun and engaging element of this activity. Older infants may begin to "take control" of the activity by covering their face and pulling the scarf away themselves while laughing!

Modification: Without using scarves, the adult can imitate a facial expression the infant has just performed to see if the facial expression is repeated again.

WHAT'S YOUR NAME?

Domain:　　*Language Development:* Orients to name
Social/Emotional Development: Interaction with caregiver

Procedure: Say the infant's name to see if they will turn their head toward you. When they look away, say their name again. If they do not look, move into their visual field as you say their name and verbally praise and smile at them for looking at you. You can move to each side of them and repeat saying their name when they are not looking at you. Always praise them looking when you say their name.

Modification: If the infant does not look at you, take an object they are looking at and move it up to your eyes as you say their name to get them to look at you. Verbally praise them and smile.

DANCE PARTY

Domain: *Physical Development:* Rocking back and forth while on all
          fours or bouncing while in a supported standing position
          Social/Emotional Development: Interaction with caregiver
          Language Development: Imitating vocalizations/singing to
          the music

Procedure: Turn on lively music and begin to dance. Encourage the infant
to dance with you. This can be done with infants who are just beginning
to crawl or from a supported standing position. Infants who are seated can
move their arms and bounce. This activity can be done with the infant in
front of the wall mirror so they can watch himself dance. A variation of this
activity could be turning the music off and on and encouraging them to start
and stop dancing with the music.

LOVE THE BABY

Domain: *Physical Development:* Imitatating simple actions
          Language Development: Receptive understanding; following
          directions
          Social/Emotional Development: Demonstrating caring ac-
          tions

Procedure: Provide a small soft doll to the child and ask them to "love" the
baby. Imitate possible actions, such as hugging, kissing, and "rocking the
baby," verbally prompting the child to copy your actions on the doll.

OBSTACLE COURSE

Domain: *Physical Development:* Navigating a variety of surfaces
          Language Development: Receptive understanding; following
          directions

Procedure: Set up a variety of surfaces for crawlers and new walkers to
navigate, to include soft surfaces, tunnels, and small blocks. For new walkers, be sure to place the course near a wall or shelf so the child can use that
surface to maintain balance.

PLANNING THE INFANT DAY

Caregivers and educational professionals who interact daily with infants
must have great perceptual and sensitive response skills because infant
development is so rapid that the needs of the various infants will change

almost on a weekly basis. For example, a group of infants of 4, 6, 9, and 12 months will exhibit very different motor, communication, and cognitive skills because their brain development during this first year is so rapid. Thus the curriculum activities and levels of behavioral challenge provided must cover a wide range during this age period.

Professionals who have a flexible range of skills themselves, including a playful approach to infant care, are especially able to promote infant developmental progress. Sometimes those who care for infants get so caught up in the essential "care" elements (e.g., feeding, diapering) that they lose their ability to respond playfully to the infants' attempts to reach out, move more actively, engage with toys and other objects, and try to initiate and respond to human interactions. It is very important that the adults who care for children in this age range are aware of the rapidly changing stages of brain development during the infant year. They must understand that it is essential for infants to have appropriate and plentiful physical interactions with the objects and other features of their environment, as well as increasingly complex social interaction with adults and peers in order to enable their brains to develop rich neuronal connections. Although it is best if infants are never placed in automatic swings, they definitely should not be left in such a swing or other device for long periods of time without human attention. Figure 2.2 shows a sample of a daily plan that incorporates responsive and challenging activities that follow developing infants' leads. Some of these should be included in every caregiving day.

HELPING PARENTS PROVIDE BRAIN-ENHANCING ENVIRONMENTS

One of the most important roles of the infant educator/caregiver is to provide parents and other home caregivers with knowledge and encouragement of practices that will enhance their infants' brain development. They can share recommendations in these ways:

1. Provide information on developmental milestones/screening tools to inform parents/caregivers of infant skills as they are emerging. This can help parents/caregivers promote these skills at home and/or to identify when their infant may need early intervention services to support development.
2. Send home to parents/caregivers daily or weekly reports of the behavioral changes and growth their infants have demonstrated and suggest ways they can interact with their infants to encourage further brain development.
3. Provide information on home environmental practices that can support infant brain development (e.g., adult/child interactive and language/sound play).

Figure 2.2. Sample Infant Day Schedule

Very young infants (0–6 months) eat/sleep on their own schedule.

8:15–8:20	Arrival and Morning Routine Activities—Center Play
8:21–8:25	Diapering/Handwashing/Transition to Breakfast
8:30–8:55	Breakfast
9:00–9:10	Language or Music Activity*
	Dance party—turn on some lively music and begin to dance to address physical development and rhythm
9:10–9:40	Outdoor Atelier and Investigations*
	Sensory play—scooping and pouring water
9:40–9:50	Transition from Outdoor Play
	Singing songs
9:55–10:05	Morning Meeting*
	Songs, finger plays, or story time
10:10–10:25	Morning Investigations*
	Making music—provide various rattles and other noise-making materials of different sizes for infant to grasp and shake
10:30–10:40	Center Play
10:45–10:55	Light and Art Investigations*
	Mirror play—place infant in front of wall mirror and/or angled floor mirrors that will encourage looking up while on stomach or that have a bar encouraging baby to pull to stand
11:00–11:10	Preparation for Lunch/Diaper Changing/Handwashing
11:10–11:20	Lunch
11:30–2:00	Nap and Rest Time
2:00–2:30	Snack with Language or Music Activity*—teacher sings songs that incorporate finger plays and encourage child participation
2:30–3:30	Outdoor Atelier and Investigations*
	Push and pull toys—encourage physical movement using push and pull toys for beginning walkers and crawlers
3:30–3:45	Transition from Outdoor Play/Diapering/Handwashing
	Singing songs
3:55–4:10	Afternoon Meeting*
	Songs, finger plays, or story time
4:10–4:30	Afternoon Investigations*
	Prepare for departure
4:30–4:40	Center Play
4:40–5:15	Departure

*Activity participation is encouraged, but not required.

4. Hold brief parent meetings in which topics related to enhancing infant brain development and other areas of development are discussed.
5. Point out adult behaviors that can impede such development (e.g., pervasive infant exposure to technological devices, long sessions in restrictive equipment such as bouncy seats, and infant neglect or harmful treatment).*

ENHANCING THE BRAIN DEVELOPMENT OF MIN, DANIEL, AND LOLA

It is important to both follow the lead of each infant in the program (each of whom will probably be at somewhat different developmental levels) and make changes that continue to respond to their brain development as well as to challenge their optimum development. During this first year, infants demonstrate through their rapidly changing behaviors that they are becoming increasingly engaged in their environment and in meeting challenges that they seek.

An environment rich in objects to see, touch, and manipulate and in people who are responsive, knowledgeable, and playful can provide essential stimulation for rich brain development. Such environments are especially important if home environments lack many activities that promote early brain development. The focus of an infant curriculum should be on playful and responsive activities that provide opportunities to address the wide variety of developmental domains initiated during the first year of life. These activities will be growth-enhancing for Min, Daniel, and Lola.

Min. The infant teacher can provide Min with a stimulating environment that challenges her to use her gross-motor, communication, fine-motor, and problem-solving skills. The introduction of brightly colored rattle toys would be interesting to Min and allow her to grasp and shake to make sounds. Her teacher could shake the toy and place it slightly out of reach to encourage Min to move toward the toy. Finding toys with moveable parts would encourage Min to use more refined motor movements and hold her attention for a longer time period. Because Min seems so attached to her teacher, she could position herself behind the toy and verbally encourage Min to move toward her. Engaging in the movement of different toys during the day will keep Min busy and engaged. Her teacher can interact with Min by engaging in vocal turn taking, repeating the sounds Min makes. She also can show excitement when Min shakes the rattle toy.

---

* Staff should have training in how to document possible infant neglect or abuse and appropriate ways to report such behaviors.

Daniel. Helping Daniel expand his musical and activity interests is important. Daniel could benefit from intentional activities to reinforce rhythm, in order to reinforce brain connections being made for music, even in infancy. Parents and other caregivers can model a steady beat when singing or playing a song to reinforce rhythm learning. They can keep a beat on his back or leg or use the child's name in a song, which adds a special element of connection to music and the caregiver. Caregivers can say or sing his name (e.g., Dan—i—el; Dan-i—el Dan-i—el) while keeping a beat on his leg or clapping or beating a drum or pot. This allows him to both *feel* the beat and *see* the hand movement, as well as *hear* the rhythmic beat and his name.

Lola. Because Lola is already very active, she needs many opportunities to expend energy and practice those skills in ways appropriate for her age level. Her parents and caregivers should ensure that a safe environment allows her to move around and practice her advancing motor skills. She also needs interesting toys/objects that she can pick up, throw, mouth, shake, and activate. Since her physical skills are advanced (and possibly her language skills), Lola might enjoy gamelike activities such as "peekaboo," hiding and finding objects, and listening to songs and repeating the sounds of words. She will soon enjoy areas for playful running and jumping. Children such as Lola are often considered "naughty" because they may open doors of low cupboards and take out pans or plates, climb on tables to get objects that are out of reach, and fuss if required to stay in a crib for long periods of time. (They also often learn to climb out of their cribs!) Lola's parents and teachers should try to appreciate the initiating qualities of children like Lola and recognize that what may often seem like inappropriate behavior is really evidence of their advancing physical, cognitive, and language skills.

QUESTIONS FOR DISCUSSION

1. What strategies can teachers use to facilitate Min's language skills and problem-solving skills? How does the battery-operated music toy compete with the development of these skills?

2. How can teachers encourage Min to explore the classroom and increase her motor skills in consideration of her love of the classroom teachers?

3. Why is it important to use animated gestures and facial expressions and make eye contact with Daniel?

4. What other ways can music and rhythmic activities be used appropriately with children of Daniel's age?

5. How should Lola's parents support her rapid motor and cognitive development and still be sure the environment is safe but responsive to her advancing developmental needs?

6. If Lola were in a care environment, how could the caregivers adapt their environment to allow Lola the freedom to explore her developing skills?

SUGGESTIONS FOR FURTHER READING/LISTENING

Bergen, D. (2018) Infant sensorimotor play: Development of socio-cultural competence and enactive cognition. In P. K. Smith & J. L. Roopnarine (Eds.), *The Cambridge handbook of play: Developmental and disciplinary perspectives* (pp. 125–141). Cambridge, United Kingdom: Cambridge University Press.

Bergen, D., Reid, R., & Torelli, L. (2009). *Educating and caring for very young children: The infant/toddler curriculum* (2nd ed.). New York, NY: Teachers College Press.

DiCarlo, C. F., Onwujuba, C., & Baumgartner, J. J. (2014). Infant communicative behaviors and maternal responsiveness. *Child and Youth Care Forum, 43*(2), 195–209.

DiCarlo, C. F., & Vagianos, L. A. (2009). Preferences and play. *Young Exceptional Children, 12*(4), 31–39.

Miss Gail's Quiet Time CD for infants is available at http://missgailmusic.com under OUR MUSIC and on streaming music platforms such as Spotify, Apple, and Amazon Music.

CHAPTER 3

Fostering Brain Development in the Toddler Curriculum

Tommy

Tommy is a 19-month-old boy who usually spends all his time at home with his mother, Janice, every day. She is now 6 months pregnant with her second baby. His father is an engineer who has a demanding job although he is home most evenings. Janice is having difficulty coping with Tommy at home, although he does very well when he is not at home. For example, he will go to other adults at his parents' church or at parties with many people, and he can quietly and easily stay for 3–4 hours in settings other than his home without needing constant attention from anyone. In fact, when he is in other care settings, he eats, sleeps, and plays so well that many people say to his parents: "What a nice baby!" Tommy has not yet started to walk well although he can pull up and stand by low tables or furniture and take a few steps. However, when he is at home alone with his mother, he often screams, cries, and throws his toys away. He doesn't want to go to bed until midnight, and his parents are not successful at putting him to sleep at bedtime. Also, they do not clearly know what he likes to do or what he is interested in playing. So far, they have not talked to their pediatrician about Tommy's home behavior, but they are planning to do so.

Miguel

Miguel is 18 months old, and he is participating for the first time with his mother in a music event in the community. When the egg shakers are given out, Miguel holds one in each hand and starts to shake them in a random fashion as the music begins. As the song continues to play, however, he sometimes is rhythmically on beat, and he moves his torso by rocking back and forth to the music rhythm. When the song calls for shaking the eggs high or low and placing them in other ways, he attempts to follow a few of these directions. Although he is not continually following directions, he does observe the others in the room who are modeling the actions, and he attempts to copy their actions. Miguel makes the scarf "dance" and bobs his head as he moves the scarf through space. He also "dances" by bouncing and moving his feet in a stomping fashion. Miguel shows that he is very aware of the music and exhibits joy in movement to music. He seems to know that he is "dancing."

Simeon

Simeon seems to love coming to Ms. Laura's preschool classroom. Every morning when he arrives, he has a big smile on his face. At 28 months, he is big for his age and really too big for the umbrella stroller that his mother uses until his "real" wheelchair comes in. Simeon has global developmental delay and low muscle tone; he is not yet moving independently or even sitting up on his own. He has just begun receiving early intervention services in the last 3 weeks, and the first priority is positioning equipment. The physical therapist, Ms. Chris, visited his home and ordered a wheelchair last week. In the classroom, there are a variety of different pieces of equipment that can be used to help Simeon interact with materials. Ms. Laura knows that with proper support of his torso, he will be better able to use his hands. The floor sitter equipment that Ms. Chris uses puts him on eye level with his peers and has both a hip strap and a bolster to keep him securely in an upright position. The tray of the floor sitter is also covered with carpet, which allows toys with velcro to stay securely attached. Simeon beams as he plays with materials surrounded by the other children.

REVIEW OF BRAIN DEVELOPMENT AT THE TODDLER AGE LEVEL

In planning toddler curriculum, it is important to consider how brain development occurs during the toddler years. Figure 3.1 gives a review of brain development information at the toddler age level.

FOSTERING BRAIN DEVELOPMENT AT THE TODDLER AGE LEVEL

Toddlers seem to be learning all the time, and sometimes they may learn things that adults wish they did not learn. Their imitative skills and their activity level may result in their attempting actions that adults do not yet think they are competent to do, such as "wash" dishes or turn on the television.

It is common for toddlers to begin to assert their own ideas and desires, and sometimes these conflict with those of adult caregivers. Adults should recognize that toddler assertion of their own ideas is evidence of their brain development; further, adults should give toddlers some activities in which

Figure 3.1. Review of Brain Development at the Toddler Age Level

- Toddler brains are two and a half times as active as adult brains. At age 2, they have as many neuronal connections (synapses) as adults do; by age 3 their brains have twice as many synaptic connections as adults have!
- The toddler brain has more neurotransmitters and a higher metabolic rate than that of adults.
- Increases in myelination, which speeds message transmission, makes the toddler brain increase in weight. By age 3 the toddler brain weighs about 3 pounds.
- The toddler's sensorimotor areas are strengthening, and the brain's hemispheric growth enables right- or left-handedness to be established.
- The parieto-temporal areas (site of perceptual and language skills) further develop, and the toddler's growth spurts are evident in areas related to language (Broca and Wernike brain areas).
- Toddlers often have a "vocabulary burst" that occurs at about 16–20 months and a later "comprehension burst" at about 30 months.
- As the cerebrum continues to develop, toddlers gain more ability to control their attention.
- By about 18 months, most toddlers can talk about events or objects that they can remember, and this development is related to maturation of the hippocampal area, medial thalamus, basal forebrain, and prefrontal cortex.
- By age 3, basic cognitive abilities such as attention and memory are maturing. Toddlers can use simple memory strategies such as repetition to remember information.
- Emotional centers in the lower limbic system gain stronger connections with the frontal lobes, and toddlers can begin to identify emotions and say when they feel "mad," "sad," "happy."
- A very important developmental milestone during toddlerhood is the ability to understand pretending. They can act "as if" they can drink pretend tea or talk to their "baby" doll. Accompanying this pretense ability is "toddler humor," and because toddlers now "know" the way some things are supposed to be, they can deliberatively make "joking play."

their ideas are welcome. An environment that supports toddler brain development, therefore, involves putting toddlers in safe but appropriately challenging environments in which they can engage in actively exploring their many developing skills. Their experiences (primarily playful ones) should be accompanied by rich and varied language environments, encouragement of mastery of both small and large motor skills, and opportunities to engage in social interactions with other children and with caring adults.

Especially important for brain development during this age period are experiences that engage toddlers in the following activities:

1. Active large and small muscle skill development
2. Repetitive language practice in songs, rhymes, and stories
3. Reading and talking about picture books and books with repetitive language
4. Object play that challenges fine motor skills and cognitive understanding
5. Safe but expanded outdoor and indoor play that encourages exploration and exercise of both fine and large motor skills
6. Replica "house" toys (pans, dishes, stove top, bed) to foster simple pretense scripts with familiar dolls, action figures, and teachers (toddlers are not usually engaged in pretense with other children)
7. Many safe riding/mobility toys and pathways
8. Safe but toddler-challenging climbing and jumping opportunities

Early-age toddlers will need more direct interaction with adult caregivers, but toddlers also need time to explore qualities of other children and to play in parallel fashion with their peers (doing similar activities with only occasional play interactions). Although toddlers still need adult monitoring, there should be some activities they can initiate by themselves and with other children. Because toddler brain synaptic growth is so rapid, their interests and activities will grow and change often (at least weekly) so teachers need to be ready to enlarge the scope and difficulty level of toys and activities often.

While some of the suggested activities involve adult initiation, in most cases the adult's role is to provide the materials, equipment, and ideas and then to be responsive to the child's actions. For example, the adult can "drink" the "milk" that the child provides, watch as the child climbs a "high" set of steps, and/or listen to the child's "story" with interest.

Because toddlers' interests change quickly, educators should expect to have a wide range of materials and activities available and to encourage the toddlers to explore, engage, and attempt to master many skills. Toddlers wish to try many activities that adults may not think they are yet capable of doing, so an important strategy for adults is to have simple versions of more complex materials and to "scaffold" children's attempts to engage in challenging tasks by observing and helping when needed. This includes "self-help" skills like self-dressing and self-feeding because even if the clothes get on backward or the dish makes a mess, it is important for toddlers to feel "agency" as effective doers and learners. The following section suggests a sample of curriculum activities that may facilitate toddler brain development. Of course, there are many other activities that also can be relevant for this development. The growth areas addressed use the NAEYC standards labels.

SAMPLE CURRICULUM ACTIVITIES
(CAN BE ADAPTED FOR PRESCHOOLERS)

MIRROR PLAY

Domain: *Physical Development:* Fine motor skills
Social/Emotional Development: Recognizing self
Creative Expression Development: Engaging in pretense

Procedure: Toddlers love to "paint" with shaving cream on the mirror for a "self-portrait" by tracing their own reflection on the mirror. It is easier when you have the mirror on the floor or the table. You can add more colors in the shaving cream so they can use various colors for their self-portraits.

OBSTACLE COURSE

Domain: *Physical Development:* Large motor and small motor control
Science Development: Spatial and body knowledge

Procedure: Various motor development items in the room (e.g., wooden steps, crawl-through barrels, stepping blocks) can be put together in an order and the toddlers can then go through the "obstacle course." This activity can be used after the toddlers have already become accustomed to using each of these motor activity items alone. It can make their use more challenging during months when outdoor play is more difficult. The config-urations and length of the course can be varied as the toddlers gain more motor and balance skills.

Get the Goody!

Domain: *Science Development:* Making predictions
Physical Development: Fine motor practice
Language Development: Following spoken language directions

Procedure: Take a high-interest object (e.g., a small toy or cheerio) and place it into a box, covering it with the lid while the child is watching. Use self-talk to explain your actions ("I'm going to put the car in the box and put on the lid."), then encourage the child to get the item from the box ("Take off the cover and get the car."). For more of a challenge, put the item in a jar with a twist lid. Praise the child's efforts.

Modification: If the child has difficulty, put the item in a clear plastic jar so they can still see the item, and follow the procedures above.

Timber!

Domain: *Physical Development:* Fine motor practice
Language Development: Using words as signals for action

Procedure: Place cubes (gradually increase number from 2 at 12–15 months to 8 by 28–31 months) in front of child and model building a tower. Encourage the child to do the same. After stacking cubes a few times and admiring the "building," shout "timber!" while knocking the tower down. Encourage the child to rebuild again, then knock down the tower.

Modification: For children with difficulty with hand–eye coordination, use bristle blocks or other types of blocks that link together and require less accuracy. For children who are preverbal or nonverbal, a voice output device can be used for the child to say "Timber!" while knocking down blocks (or signaling the adult to knock down the blocks for them).

Storyteller

Domain: *Physical Development:* Fine motor skill development
Early Literacy Development: Picture reading

Procedure: Present the child with a cardboard book and encourage them to "read" the book to dolls/stuffed animals while turning the pages. Encourage the child to point to pictures and talk about what is on each page while "reading" to the dolls/stuffed animals. For an older child, invert the book when handing it to them to see if he turns the book to correctly orient the picture. If he does not, say, "Oh, no! Your book is upside down!" and turn the book over.

Modification: Place small sponges between pages to assist children in putting fingers between pages in order to turn each page. Use a cookbook holder to hold the book while the child "reads" and turns the pages.

Book Maker

Domain: *Physical Development:* Fine motor skills
Language Development: Describing picture
Early Literacy Development: Writing "stories"

Procedure: Place a piece of paper in front of the child and fold it in half to make a "book." Give the child a piece of paper and ask them to make a book. Provide the child with crayons or markers to "write" their own story. After the child has finished, ask them to tell you about their picture and write down what they say. Paper/crayon developmental steps include spontaneous scribbling, imitating scribbles and crayon strokes, scribbling in circular motion, copying circles, putting "eyes" and "mouth" in a circle.

Modification: For children who have difficulty with two-handed tasks, stabilize the paper by taping it to the table.

Night Night Baby

Domain: *Physical Development:* Early pretend motions
Social/Emotional Development: Demonstrating caring action

Procedure: Demonstrate rocking a baby to sleep. Hand the doll to the child and encourage them to imitate your actions. Then ask the child to feed the baby and put them to bed. (Imitate one-step action 12–15 months; multiple step actions 24–27 months.)

Modification: Place the doll on a table in front of the child if they have difficulty holding the doll, and model how to rock and feed the doll while it is on the table surface.

Washing the Dishes

Domain: *Physical Development:* Imitating pretend actions
Social/Emotional Development: Learning social behaviors
Cognitive development: Imitating model from memory

Procedure: Present the child with some play materials needed for washing dishes (e.g., dishes, pretend soap, sponge, and towel). Ask the child to show you how mom and dad wash the dishes.

Sing a song about washing dishes and/or talk to the child about washing and drying the dishes after dinner.

Modification: If the child has difficulty completing a multistep sequence within the activity, imitate the action and/or provide a verbal prompt on what the child might do next.

SETTING THE TABLE

Domain: *Physical Development:* Imitating pretend actions
               Social/Emotional Development: Learning social behaviors
               Early Mathematics: Learning concept of one; one to one correspondence

Procedure: Before a meal, give the child several of an item needed for the meal (e.g., spoon). Go around the table with the child and ask them to give you "one" of the item and then place it on the table. Do this until all the spoons have been placed on the table. Depending on the child's interest, you could repeat this activity with other items needed for the meal. After you have demonstrated this a number of times, the child can do the placement at each place.

COLORS IN THE ART CENTER

Domain: *Language Development:* Matching objects by color name
               Creative Expression/Art Appreciation: Gaining color sensitivity

Procedure: In your art center, have different-colored containers to store crayons. After children have used the crayons, encourage them to return the crayons to the matching colored container. As you put your crayons back, use self-talk to describe your actions ("I'm going to put the red crayon back in the red container").

Modification: For younger children, limit the field of containers to a lower number to help them to be more successful in matching their crayon to the appropriate container.

What Do You Want?

Domain: *Language Development:* Using two different words meaningfully and in two- and three-word sentences

Procedure: During a meal or snack, place items within view of the child, but out of reach. Name all of the items you have for the meal or snack while holding them up ("I have crackers, cheese, and apple juice") and wait for the child to indicate what they would like. If they do not make a request, ask the child what they would like. Rather than serve the food, allow the child to request items.

Modification: If the child is preverbal or nonverbal, teach the child the sign language for "want." When you hold up each item, give the child the item if they sign for "want." For older nonverbal children, model multiple word sentences using sign language (e.g., "want cookie").

Sleep and Wake

Domain: *Physical Development:* Pulling off clothing; putting shoes on; putting on simple clothes without assistance

Procedure: In preparation for nap time, ask children to take off their shoes and socks before getting on their nap mat. Upon waking from nap, ask children to put on their socks and shoes, providing assistance in shoe tying if needed.

Modification: For children with fine motor delay, shoes with Velcro closures can be used in place of laces for greater independence.

Next!

Domain: *Language Development:* Following simple directions; using two-word sentences
Social/Emotional Development: Discriminating between boys and girls

Procedure: Adult will prompt child to tell another child it is their turn to come to an activity, such as toileting ("your turn") or meals ("come eat"). Adult will prompt child to tell a friend it is their turn for an activity and accompany the child to approach another child. The adult can ask the child to select a boy or a girl to tell.

Modification: Use photos of different children to help the child make a choice. For preverbal or nonverbal children, use a voice output device to say "your turn" after the child approaches his peer.

Song and Dance

Domain: *Language Development:* Imitating new words
        Physical Development: Imitating body movements; controlling actions
        Creative Expression/Arts Appreciation: Learning musical themes and actions

Procedure: Sing familiar songs with young children that have recurrent lyrics, such as "Twinkle, Twinkle Little Star." The recurrent lines will help them remember the words, enabling them to sing along. Adding movements to recurrent lyrics allows children who are preverbal or nonverbal to participate and provides a cognitive cue that will help children remember the words. The use of motor movements can also be used to help children request a favorite song.

Modification: If a child has difficulty performing a motor movement, provide hand-over-hand assistance to help them initiate the hand movement; it may be easier for the child to continue the movement than to initiate it.

Throw It!

Domain: *Physical Development:* Throwing overhand

Procedure: The adult will model throwing a small ball overhand. The adult will then give the small ball to the child and ask him to throw it to them. The adult and child can alternate throwing to each other and requesting the other to "throw it!" Additionally, the adult can draw a circle on the sidewalk with chalk to aim for or provide a small bucket to throw into.

Modification: Use a bean bag if the child has difficulty maintaining grasp on a ball.

Where'd It Go?

Domain: *Early Mathematics:* Finding hidden objects; object permanence
        Language Development: Responding to simple directions

Procedure: While the child is looking, cover a favorite toy with a cloth, ask them "Where'd the ___ go?," then remove the cloth to reveal the toy. Then cover the toy again, this time asking the child to "find the toy" or "pick up the cloth." If the child does not uncover the toy, show them again. Praise them for finding the toy and continue the game, as long as they are interested.

Modification: You can use "least-to-most prompting" to help the child find the toy. If they do not uncover it when given a verbal prompt ("pick up the cloth"), you can take the child's hand and physically assist them in picking up the cloth, praising them for finding the toy. Be sure to give them a chance to move the cloth independently each time, only providing physical assistance when needed.

BALLS ARE FOR THROWING!

Domain: *Physical Development:* Exploring objects by throwing
Social/Emotional Development: Interacting with caregiver; turn-taking
Language Development: Using reaching and vocalizations to communicate

Procedure: It is common for young children to explore materials by shaking, banging, and throwing objects. When children are interested in throwing, have small soft vinyl balls available to present to redirect them. Small balls are a good size to grasp and you can encourage children to throw and roll and then retrieve the ball to continue the game. You can encourage the child to take turns with you throwing and retrieving the toy.

I CAN DO IT MYSELF!

Domain: *Early Literacy:* Using objects correctly when asked
Social/Emotional Development: Interacting with caregiver
Language Development: Engaging in vocal turn taking

Procedure: Present the toddler with common objects (e.g., hairbrush) and ask them to brush their hair. This can be done in front of a mirror so toddlers can watch themselves perform the action. Provide verbal praise on the child's efforts. Repeat with other common or pretend play objects (e.g., toy phone, cup) encouraging the toddler to use the object correctly. Provide praise and reply to any communication made by the toddler to encourage conversation.

Modification: You can model how to use the material or provide physical assistance to guide the toddler to perform the correct action, providing verbal praise to reinforce the toddler's actions.

GOING ON A PICTURE WALK

Domain: *Early Literacy:* Looking at pictures when they are named
               Language Development: Trying to repeat words

Procedure: Provide the toddler a choice of two books, allowing them to choose. Read the book to the toddler, asking them at different points in the story to find pictures of items as you name them. Repeat the name and encourage them to repeat it. Verbally praise the toddler for effort. Read the book again, if they show continued interest.

MOVING MAN

Domain: *Early Literacy:* Following directions; problem solving
               Physical Development: Carrying and picking up small items

Procedure: Provide a variety of small blocks and a bucket. Encourage the child to pick up the blocks and move them to another area of the room, perhaps to use them with a truck in another area. This activity promotes both fine and gross motor skills and problem solving in the transfer of multiple small items to another location for another purpose. Encourage the child to transfer the blocks into the back of the truck and interact with them as they make decisions about how to interact with these materials.

Modification: You can use "least-to-most prompting" to help the child perform any of the above actions. If they do not begin to pick up the blocks when given a verbal prompt ("put the blocks in the container"), you can take the child's hand and physically assist them in putting the blocks in the container, praising them for picking up. Be sure to initially give them a chance to perform an action independently each time, only providing physical assistance when needed.

I DON'T WANT THAT!

Domain: *Language Development:* Expressing a preference verbally
               Social/Emotional Development: Interacting with caregiver;
                    choice making

Procedure: Provide the toddler with lots of opportunities to make choices throughout the day. Be sure that when you present a choice, there is truly an option for the toddler to say "no." You can begin by selecting two items—one that is preferred by the toddler and another that is not preferred. Present both items to the toddler and, upon presentation, ask them if they want the item. Honor when the toddler says "no" and provide them with the selected material. Think about opportunities during the day to allow the toddler to express a preference—when it is okay to say "no."

CAN YOU GET IT?

Domain: *Social/Emotional Development:* Using help in problem solving
Language Development: Using language to ask for assistance
Physical Development: Using fine motor skills

Procedure: Place a desired item, such as a small toy or Cheerio, into a clear container with a lid. Model for the child how to open the container, then place the lid back on and give it to the child. If they have difficulty, you can hold out your hand and tell them you will help if they need help. Only provide assistance if the child communicates to you in some way (e.g., handing you the container or looking at you while vocalizing/verbalizing). If they seem frustrated, you can provide physical assistance to guide them to hand the object to you while repeating your offer of assistance. Provide the child with physical assistance to guide them in opening the container and retrieving the toy or Cheerio. Repeat if the child continues to be interested.

PLANNING THE TODDLER DAY

The toddler years are ones of exponential growth in every area of development and often adults are not ready for such rapid changes in children's abilities and behaviors. Because the toddler brain is making new synaptic connections on an almost daily basis, toddlers will be doing new actions, saying new language, and demanding new emotional understanding very frequently. The most important skills that the toddler educator must have are the ability to adapt and change the environment and activities and the ability to respond to the variety of behaviors that various toddlers will demonstrate. The curriculum, therefore, must be planned with knowledge of the ways toddler brain growth occurs and how that growth is demonstrated in the activities, language, and behavioral challenges that toddlers exhibit. The playfulness that is needed for infant care and education is also very important for toddler care and education, and, in fact, it becomes even more important as toddlers age. The advice that infant caregivers should not get too caught up in "care" elements applies even more so to those working with toddlers.

Figure 3.2 shows a sample of a daily plan that incorporates responsive and challenging activities that follow the developing toddlers' leads. This age period is one that should be interesting and exciting for both children and adults.

Figure 3.2. Sample Toddler Day Schedule

7:15–8:40	Arrival and Morning Activities
8:40–8:45	Cleanup Transition
8:45–9:15	Breakfast Served Family Style
9:15–9:30	Toileting/Music and Movement
9:30–9:40	Morning Meeting
	Teachers sing a morning song with children and engage children in a short conversation, book, or music activity (varies based on age and attention span)
	Discuss project on balls, focusing on characteristics (e.g., size, color, weight)
9:40–10:30	Outdoor Atelier and Investigations
	Children may choose from a variety of play areas and have the opportunity to engage in a variety of gross motor activities.
	Children practice adult-mediated turn taking by rolling balls back and forth with peers or adults.
10:30–11:10	Indoor Atelier and Investigations (Examples)
	Explore provocations (newly introduced items (e. g., picture, leaf) brought in to spark children's interests and generate conversation, develop project work, dramatic play, blocks, sensory table, playdough, art, or engage in ball painting. Children can experiment with painting by dipping balls in paint and putting them into the top of a cardboard box and shifting the box tops from side to side to roll the painted balls to make designs on paper.
11:10–11:15	Cleanup/Water Break
11:15–11:30	Toileting/Book Time
	Read *Ball* by Mary Sullivan, a story about a dog playing catch by himself and having a dream about balls and playing catch.
11:30–12:00	Lunch
12:00–12:05	Children Prepare for Nap Time
	Help children take off shoes and prepare for rest
12:05–2:00	Nap and Rest Time
2:05–2:15	Wake Up from Nap/Restroom/Transition to Snack
	Help children put on shoes and prepare for snack
2:15–2:30	Snack Time
2:30–3:15	Outdoor Atelier and Investigations
	Continue balls study with larger balls and large buckets to practice throwing.
3:15–4:00	Indoor Atelier and Investigations
	Ramps are available for children to experiment with rolling balls and talk about concepts of "fast" and "slow."
4:00–4:10	Cleanup/Handwashing/Diapering/Toileting

Figure 3.2. Sample Toddler Day Schedule, *Continued*
_____

4:10–4:30   Enrichment Activity

                Enrichment activities will vary daily. They may include a music activity, art activity, literacy activity, and so on. Please see the posted lesson plan.

                Sing "Ball Song" by Katie Cutie Kids TV while bouncing balls or tapping balloons (be aware of latex allergies).

4:45–5:15   Table Activities/Snack/Prepare to Go Home

The greatest quality that toddler educators must have is flexibility, because toddler interests and skills change on an almost daily basis. Adults who care for children in this age range need to be especially aware of the fact that toddler behaviors, language, and cognitive interests change and grow rapidly because toddler brain development, particularly in relation to growth in the higher brain centers, is extensive. Toddlers' challenging physical interactions with objects and other environmental features and their interests and playful interactions with peers and adults are the means by which they develop rich neuronal connections. Adults should take the role of "facilitators" of toddler behavioral initiation and be sure that there are many safe, interesting, and appropriately challenging opportunities for toddler engagement with the environment.

ENHANCING THE BRAIN DEVELOPMENT OF
TOMMIE, MIGUEL, AND SIMEON

Because the toddler years are ones of great growth in brain synaptic connections, educators and parents of children in this age range have a great opportunity to foster that growth through their provision of positive and wide-ranging activities. Adults often remark on how quickly toddlers pick up on ideas and behaviors to which they are exposed (sometimes including those ideas and behaviors that adults do not want them to learn). Toddlers also are beginning to show their activity preferences through their length of attention and expressed enjoyment of such activities. Thus Tommy, Miguel, and Simeon will benefit by educator attention to the following recommendations.

Tommy: Tommy seems to be in the stage of "testing water" to gain his control, which is not unusual for toddlers. He can explore the boundaries of his strengths, experiences, and abilities to understand himself and the world around him including his family. Because of these attempts, he may express himself and his frustration through negative and somewhat aggressive behaviors such as screaming, crying, and throwing toys. Parents should fully

recognize his limited and undeveloped verbal communication skills and support him to express himself in an appropriate way with a concrete and firm direction. For instance, they can continually tell him, "I see how upset you are. But it is not a good way for you to do this. Do you want something else to play with? Then, please show me what you want to play and please do not throw this toy like that." In addition, parents should check his daily schedule to know the reasons why he doesn't go to sleep before midnight. He may need more activities, less nap time, more nutritional meals, or more comfort support when he is going to bed. The parents should also dim out lights at home and provide a quiet space for him until he is asleep. This type of interaction will enhance his brain development in a way that his needs are met with parents' or caregivers' help and responses. It will also encourage him to learn self-regulation to express his feelings and deal with challenges.

Miguel: Consistent use of music activities throughout the day, including at transitions and in singing experiences, will help Miguel's brain development for music and promote "Primary Music Development," which is the ability to sing a song in tune and keep a steady beat (see Guilmartin & Levinowitz, 2009). As educators continue to model a "steady beat" through instruments, dance, clapping, and other large movement rhythmic activities, Miguel's brain connections for rhythm will increase. As he learns to keep a steady beat, he will eventually learn more complex beats. Before children can mimic more complex rhythms, they must be able to keep a steady beat, so this is a very important step. Similarly, helping Miguel learn to match one pitch by modeling this will be helpful in making brain connections for tonality and he will eventually be able to sing a "string" of pitches in tune (which is singing a melody or song). According to Guilmartin and Levinowitz (2009), music activities help to support the development of executive functions, and consistency each day over the long term is important. If continued for Miguel throughout his toddler and preschool years, his brain connections for music will be strong and will translate into strengths for other kinds of learning.

Simeon: Providing appropriate positioning equipment for Simeon is critical to help maximize his potential for learning. When Simeon's torso is well-supported, he is better able to use his hands to explore materials. Positioning equipment that puts him at eye level with peers is also a consideration for his social development. He should rotate between sitting on the floor, at a table, and in a standing position throughout the day in order to spend time with peers participating in classroom activities. Teachers should be attentive to stabilizing materials for him (e.g., paper when drawing, his bowl when eating, and toys while playing) to aid in his interaction with materials. These strategies help Simeon function in the toddler classroom and prevent secondary disabilities, such as skeletal issues from poor positioning, poor fine motor skills from lack of experience with materials, and poor social skills from lack of opportunities to interact with peers.

QUESTIONS FOR DISCUSSION

1. In what ways could Tommy's parents have more attentive interaction with him to understand his interests in playing?
2. If Miguel's teacher does not think his or her own musical ability is great, should that be a reason to ignore musical development in the classroom?
3. How can teachers encourage Simeon to interact with a variety of materials while he is in positioning equipment?
4. How can teachers facilitate peer interaction between Simeon and his classmates?

SUGGESTIONS FOR FURTHER READING

Bankston, J., & DiCarlo, C. (2020). Building self-esteem in toddlers: The sociocultural context. *Early Years, 40*(1), 26–28.

Bergen, D., & Raver, S. (1999). Techniques for infants and toddlers who are at risk. In S. Raver, *Intervention strategies for infants and toddlers: A team approach* (2nd. ed., pp. 198–223). Upper Saddle River, NJ: Merrill.

CHAPTER 4

Fostering Brain Development in the Preschool Curriculum

Jesús

A 4½-year-old boy, Jesús, has a dual language background in both Spanish and English. He lives with his mom, a younger sister, and an older brother; however, his father was recently deported. The family arrived in the United States 2 years ago, and, according to his mother, he and his family are anxious to learn English and the American way of life. Jesús has been in a state-funded preschool program for a year, but he has very low literacy in both English and Spanish. Although he was referred for a hearing and speech pathology assessment and has been receiving therapy for several months, there as yet has been little improvement in his literacy development, even in his native language. When receiving instruction in English, he is often quiet and relies on his Spanish-speaking peers to help him through the activity. In addition, his actual learning time with peers is often cut short due to his aggressive behaviors in class, which result in his being removed from the activity.

Ruby

Ruby is a 3½-year-old girl who is usually very quiet in group activities, and she often does not participate in many activities, including music activities. When the teacher plays the "jumping" song, however, she does begin to stand up and move since bouncing and jumping is an activity that comes "naturally" to most children and does not require them to decide how to do it or if they are doing it correctly. She jumps and bounces to most of the song, joining into the activity along with her peers. The song also helps to hone her gross motor skills and the rhythmic jumping reinforces keeping a "beat" with large movement. Jumping also provides physical exercise even though Ruby does not realize she is getting physical exercise. To Ruby, this is just fun because it feels natural to bounce and jump. As the music activities continue during the next weeks, the teacher observes that Ruby is making more attempts to respond to other active movement songs, and she is acting more comfortable within the preschool classroom in general.

Billy

Billy's mother, Shelby, is pleased that her son has been accepted into the 3–4-year-old mixed-age class at the neighborhood child-care center. She had been concerned that his diagnosis of Down syndrome might prevent him from attending the same child-care center that her older son, Max, had attended. At 3 years old, Billy has some intelligible two-word sentences and uses a variety of conventional gestures to make his needs known. He is a happy-go-lucky child who goes with the flow. His gross motor skills are good enough for him to get where he wants to go, but he is still a little unsure on uneven surfaces, or going up stairs, and has not yet mastered a pedal trike. He also has some trouble with his grasp and potty training. Shelby noticed that Billy always seems happy enough to enter the classroom each morning, but each afternoon when she picks him up, he does not seem to be doing anything worthwhile. While the teachers report that he is no trouble, Shelby is concerned that Billy is just "hanging out," and because he isn't a behavior problem he might not be getting the attention he needs. She knows the early years are important for Billy's development, but she feels she might be sacrificing social interaction at the expense of other important developmental skills.

REVIEW OF BRAIN DEVELOPMENT AT THE PRESCHOOL AGE LEVEL

In planning preschool curriculum, it is important to consider how brain development occurs during the preschool years. Figure 4.1 gives a review of brain development information at the preschool age level.

CURRICULUM PRIORITIES AT THE PRESCHOOL AGE LEVEL

Although many families do provide enriching environments that enhance their preschool children's brain development, there are also many families whose children come to preschool from environments that do not provide many brain network stimulating experiences. For example, these children may not hear elaborated language at home, visit interesting local sites such as libraries or farms, take trips on buses or airplanes, or go to music or art events. Some environments may even disrupt brain development by fostering more connections in the children's fear or anger-inducing brain centers.

**Figure 4.1. Review of Brain Development at the Preschool Age Level
    (ages 4 to 5)**

- During the preschool age period, there is rapid growth of the brain's communication systems, with neuronal connections (synaptogenesis) occurring very rapidly.
- The preschool child's brain is very active, and the metabolic rates of glucose utilization are two times the normal adult levels.
- The speed of brain action also is being increased by the myelination (covering the neuron networks with an insulation sheath) of neuronal networks.
- Refinements are taking place in the fine and gross motor, sensory, and language areas of the brain and these sensorimotor parieto-temporal areas have high blood flow.
- There are fast growth rates in frontal lobe areas regulating ability to plan new actions.
- Frontal lobe development fosters awareness of where and when something was learned (source memory) and increases their ability to regulate planning of new actions.
- Preschoolers require activation of many brain regions to complete cognitive tasks.
- Their attentional networks are strengthened when they are taught various skills. For example, with music training, they may gain auditory selective attention.
- Their extensive and elaborated pretend play enhances "theory of mind" and strengthens synaptic networks related to cognitive, language, and social development.
- Because preschool brain development is a time of dynamic action that emphasizes brain growth and maturation, children will benefit from exposure to a wide range of positive and growth-enhancing experiences.
- At later ages this brain "construction" will be pruned and become more specialized.
- The more experiential connections the brain has developed during this age period, the richer and more competent the initial and later pruning process will be.

Thus, the experiences provided in the preschool for these children may be especially important for enhancing their positive brain network connecting processes. Experiences that involve the "whole body" are still important because every action and experience may strengthen important physical, cognitive, social, and emotional brain areas.

Preschoolers should be given many opportunities to "do it myself!" Especially important for brain development during this age period are experiences that engage them in the following activities:

1. Learning to make music with a variety of instruments, to "dance" to different rhythms, and to sing songs with simple lyrics. It is

important for music experiences to be "active." Although listening to songs on a CD or video is fine, that activity can be taken to a "next step" by having children dance to songs and/or replicate what they know by singing familiar songs.

2. Interacting with other children on many play experiences, tasks, or activities.
3. Book "reading" both by the teacher and by the children (simple stories with pictures are ideal for child "reads").
4. Practicing motor skills to help them gain confidence and "expert" performance (e.g., jumping off sturdy platforms, climbing safe structures, pedaling three-wheel bikes; cutting with scissors).
5. Engaging in elaborate object play with toys and materials that can be used in many different ways (e.g., puzzles, blocks of different types, playdough).
6. Using a full range of "pretend" materials (e.g., clothes that replicate worker types; fancy, beautiful materials; home and work replica objects).
7. Performing "helper" activities in which children do tasks for teachers or other children (e.g., clean-up time; washing tables).

By preschool age, many classroom activities should build on children's independence and growing competence, and adults should provide this "room to grow" over the course of the school year. Because preschoolers have a wide range of growing skills, their experiences should help them gain confidence in their abilities and in their own initiatives and ideas for play and for learning. The preschool teacher should be especially aware of individual children's interests and abilities and should plan options that enable all children to feel both challenged and successful. It is especially important for early childhood educators to ignore "pseudo-knowledge" about brain enhancement, such as using curriculum supposedly designed for "right-brain or left-brain" activities or focusing on the children's hypothesized "learning styles." Educators need to involve children's "whole brain" in rich learning experiences and give young children opportunities to participate in many varied and interesting types of experiences to stimulate their optimum brain development. Early childhood educators who provide interesting and appropriately challenging curriculum activities have a very important role in enhancing the healthy brain development of all preschool children.

The following section suggests a sample of curriculum activities that may facilitate preschool children's brain development. Of course, there are many other activities that also can be relevant for this development. The growth areas addressed use the NAEYC standards labels.

SAMPLE CURRICULUM ACTIVITIES (CAN BE ADAPTED FOR TODDLERS OR KINDERGARTEN/PRIMARY CHILDREN)

ALL ABOUT MY BODY

Domain: *Language Development:* Using names of body parts
Early Literacy: Expressive language related to body part labels
Social/Emotional Development: Self-awareness; self-comparisons of own characteristics to those of others

Procedure: Teacher introduces topic by asking some questions and listening to what children say in order to gather students' previous knowledge about themselves and their bodies: "What is special about you?" "What parts of you are different from or similar to the others?" Then the teacher introduces the vocabulary words of the body parts by using a picture of each part and asking students if they know the name of that body part. Colors and other adjectives (e.g., big, small, long, and short) can be added in Spanish and English. Then the teacher places an image on the board and writes the English and Spanish word next to it. When all words have been introduced, the teacher encourages children to identify the words in relation to their bodies (use specific vocabulary to describe the parts). Then the class reads a book about body parts and the self (e.g., *Stand Tall, Molly Lou Melon* by Patty Lovell; *What I like About Me* by Allia Zobel Nolan; *I like Myself!* by Karen Beaumont); students are encouraged to ask questions about the story. Finally, children can create themselves in a drawing, painting, or with playdough. When they are done, the teacher documents what they did by taking photos and recording a short story or interview.

Modification: For children who are nonverbal, a voice output device can be used with vocabulary that helps them to participate in the discussion and stories. For children with fine motor difficulty, tape can be used to stabilize paper. Using an elevated surface can help children with postural instability (e.g., using a 3-inch binder to create a slanted surface). Thicker writing instruments or foam grips (e.g., pipe insulation or a foam hair curler) can assist children with grasp.

USING MATH TO MAKE PARFAITS

Domain: *Early Mathematics:* Recognize, copy, and extend patterns
           Social/Emotional Development: Develop positive self-identity
           and sense of belonging; describe feelings

Procedure: The teacher will demonstrate making a parfait for snack using two different flavors of yogurt, two different kinds of diced fruit, and granola or grape-nuts cereal in a layered pattern. After the teacher demonstrates, the children will have access to the foods and will be guided to build their own parfait, following the pattern demonstrated by the teacher or by creating their own pattern. Children can either follow the teacher's pattern or can plan their pattern on paper before creating. Children will be asked to share their pattern before enjoying their snack.

Modification: Adults can use picture cues to provide step-by-step instructions to assist children with completing multiple-step actions after the adult has presented the activity.

FLOATING SCARVES

Domain: *Physical Development:* Body awareness; fine and gross motor
           skills
           Creative Expression/Arts Appreciation: Understanding of
           rhythm and beat

Procedure: Scarves give children freedom to "create" their own fun while dancing and moving. No real instruction is necessary. Allowing the freedom is important, and even children with special needs or who are generally reserved will find "something" to do with the scarf or some way to move. The scarf often gives some confidence and distraction from anxiety and fear of moving or expressing themselves in a group. The teacher can also make the scarves "dance" to the beat and model ways to move the scarf, such as large circles, up and down, face the child and play "peekaboo" to the beat of the song, throw the scarves in the air and try to catch them. Use varied types of music, some of which encourages faster actions and some that encourages slower actions.

When the song is over, the teacher can tell the children to hide their faces or just model it and sing "peek-aaaaaaaaaaa-" on the pitch of the song for as long as you can and then . . . "BOO!" Have the children hide the scarves by squishing them as small as they can in their hands. The teacher can hide by bending over and hiding her or his face (and have the children do the same) and do the same activity, but on "BOO" come back up and throw the scarves in the air! Scarves should be small enough for children to handle, no larger than 24" x 24", and of a light material such as nylon or chiffon. However, varieties may include different colors and multicolored scarves.

Modification: For children with difficulty grasping, a hair tie can be sewn onto the end of a scarf, allowing the scarf to be worn on the child's wrist. For a child with limited motor movement, a fan with streamers operated by a switch could be placed in front of the child, allowing them to turn the fan off and on while the music is playing.

CARING FOR THE GARDEN

Domain: *Science:* Using scientific inquiry; acquiring specific knowledge related to life science (properties of living things)
Early Mathematics: Understanding ways of representing numbers and relationships between numbers and quantities

Procedure: Teacher reads *What Does a Seed Need?* by Liz Goulet Dubois to begin a conversation of what plants need to grow. The teacher then leads the children in the planting of small plants into pots and describes the jobs children will need to do to care for the plants (e.g., water them daily, move them into the sun). The teacher uses measuring cups and directs the children to take four scoops of dirt to fill their pot, put the plant in, press down the soil, and then water with a small cup of water. She identifies the four main parts of a plant (roots, stem, leaves, seeds) and encourages children to gently touch each part as they discuss. As the children finish planting, the teacher revisits the book to remind the children of what the plant needs to grow (e.g., sunlight, water) and demonstrates how to measure the size of their plant with a ruler and record its size. The children will record the size of their plants each week using a ruler and writing the number on a chart.

Modification: A picture chart can be used to sequence events in the activity for children with attention deficits or to correspond to the story, allowing children to demonstrate comprehension.

Birthday Party

Domain: *Cognitive Development:* Choosing a multistep task and completing it on their own
Early Literacy: Developing familiarity with writing implements, conventions, and communication skills through written representations, symbols, and letters

Procedure: The teacher will include props in the dramatic play area for children to have a birthday party, including a picture book about a birthday party. Children will have choices in a variety of birthday party–related tasks, such as writing invitations, baking a cake, decorating the area, wrapping presents, and singing happy birthday. If multiple children are interested in participating, children can decide on roles each will play, including birthday boy/girl, mom/ dad, party planner, and so on.

Modification: For children who have difficulty with delayed imitation, a prerecorded video can be used to demonstrate a short play sequence using materials available in the classroom for the birthday party scheme. This video should be short in length (1–2 minutes) and shown immediately before the children enter the dramatic play center where the materials are available (see Bellini & Akullian, 2007, for a review).

Engaging in Active Music

Domain: *Creative Expression/Arts Appreciation:* Music and song elaboration
Language Development: Gaining vocabulary and sound discrimination
Physical Development: Whole-body active movement
Cognitive Development: Increased conceptual understanding

Procedure: One of the most important things teachers can encourage in the classroom is "child active" music participation, not simply having children absorb music in a passive sense. Music activities that provide "something to do" instead of just watching or listening are valuable. Often, teachers feel most comfortable beginning to use music more effectively by presenting in new ways songs the children already know. While introducing songs other than "standards" is absolutely necessary, taking a children's "standard" and evolving it into a participatory song can be a great way for teachers to start "being musical" throughout the day. An example is the "Muffin Man" song, which can be turned into the "Muffin Man Mix-Up!" After singing it the traditional way, ask for ideas of what a child had for breakfast or their favorite food. The teacher can come up with the "answer" in the song, but usually children will come up with ideas on their own, depending on the developmental level. It does not have to "make sense." Some possible responses might be:

> Do you know the apple man, the apple man, the apple man?
> Do you know the apple man? Where does the apple man live?
> He lives on Orchard Lane!

Another child might say . . . spaghetti!

> Do you know the spaghetti man, the spaghetti man, the spaghetti man?
> Do you know the spaghetti man? . . . where does the spaghetti man live?
> He lives in ITALY!!! . . . Or on Pasta Lane . . . or in The Spaghetti House . . . on Tomato Sauce Lane!

The ideas go on and on. Just take the first one and sing it! Then go on, giving any child who wishes to participate the chance to add. If they do not choose to participate in a music activity, they are still engaged with their brains. "Participation" in music activities is also being accomplished through observing and listening.

Modification: For children who may be nonverbal, the teacher could have two dice with picture cues paired with words on each side (total of six words per die). One die for *foods* and another die for *street names*. When it is the target child's turn to name something, he can roll the dice to participate in the song.

DEVELOPING AND ENGAGING IN A MOTOR MAZE

Domain: *Physical Development:* Large muscle control and coordination of movements in upper and/or lower body.
Language Development: Learning to interpret symbolic directions
Social Studies: Identifying workers and their roles as citizens within the community

Procedure: Children will use chalk and other outdoor props to create a maze for ride-on toys. Chalk will be available for children to draw roads on the concrete for ride-on toys. Various signs (e.g., to indicate direction of traffic, stop signs, yield signs, stop lights) will be used to direct traffic while children use a variety of gross motor skills to ride on tricycles, scooters, wiggle cars, or hop bouncers or push baby strollers. Children will determine rules and assign roles (e.g., traffic cop, crossing guard, mom/dad), including giving tickets to drivers who do not stay on the road or go the wrong way.

Modification: An adapted riding car or bike with a harness and hip restraints can be used by children with motor deficits to allow proper positioning while riding around the obstacle course. The teacher can assist the child in moving through the course by following her directions to "stop" and "go." A voice output device can be used for these verbal commands for nonverbal children.

CREATING VISUAL ARTS

Domain: *Creative Expression/Arts Appreciation:* Appreciate visual arts, creating various forms of visual arts from different cultures.
Social/Emotional Development: Gaining positive self-identity, sense of belonging; describing self, characteristics, preferences, thoughts, and feelings

Procedure: Children will read a book about the work of Van Gogh; the teacher will provide several paintings of his work in the classroom to serve as inspiration pieces. A variety of paints and brushes will be available for children to use to make their interpretation of a Van Gogh–style painting. Children will be asked to name characteristics of the Van Gogh paintings they like and to describe their painting to the class.

Modification: Paper can be taped onto a wall to allow children to stand while painting. Children with physical disabilities can use a standing frame in order to paint on the wall.

JUMPING TO MUSIC

Domain: *Physical Development:* Body control of large muscles
Creative Expression/Art Appreciation: Rhythm development
Cognitive Development: Following subtle directions

Procedure: Gross motor movement skills are those that require whole-body movement and involve the large muscles of the body. When a lively song is played, even without direction, the average 3-year-old child has the skills to jump in place with both feet together. Each time the music stops, the children also are to stop jumping. When the music starts again, they resume jumping. As long as the teacher keeps the "jumping beat" and bounces with the upper part of his body, there is no need for extreme jumping motions by the teacher. Teachers can use their own discretion on modifying their own large movement activity and their movements do not need to be as exact or as active as the children's movements. As long as children see the teacher smiling, singing, and "moving" in some way, they will enjoy jumping. Older preschoolers and kindergartners are generally able to jump and freeze on cue.

Modification: For children with motor impairment, this activity can be modified for children to stomp their feet or tap the table while in a seated position.

A Walk Around the Block

Domain: *Science Development:* Environmental knowledge; categorization; memory
Social/Emotional Development: Following complex social rules; concern for other participants
Physical Development: Large motor strength and endurance; small motor skills

Procedure: Before the walk the teacher will engage the children in thinking about what they might see if they were taking a walk in the preschool neighborhood. (Note: There may be *some* neighborhoods too dangerous for this walking trip, but most preschools will be able to do this activity, even if they are located in older or urban neighborhoods.) After asking, "What do you think we might see if we take a walk in our neighborhood?" the teacher will make a list of things the children suggest (even if some are not practical). Then the group will review the list, and the children can think about what they might be looking for as they walk. After reviewing safety concerns (holding hands, walking in pairs, following the teacher, and so on) the group will take the walk. As they walk, children can call out what they see and try to remember the items to talk about later. Both natural and human-made objects or scenes can be identified. Although some objects or scenes may not be "child-appropriate," if they are part of the child's neighborhood, they can be talked about. When they return, children can draw pictures or make up stories about what they saw. (Talking about strange or scary things helps one not to be worried or scared.)

Alternative ways to take this walk would be the following:

1. Just 4–6 children take the walk on different days and report what they see to the class.
2. The class could take a walk in a park.
3. The class could take a walk around the school playground area.
4. The class could take an actual "field trip" to a park, farm, or other venue.

The important aspect is that the children will use their observation skills to identify features of their environment and be able to talk about these features. Good observational skills are essential for every person and such activities are important for activating brain networks.

Modification: Children who have physical disabilities can ride in a wagon (or wheelchair) to participate in the "walk." Picture cues can be added to the list to help the children "read" the list as they are walking.

LEARNING THE CALENDAR MONTHS

Domain: *Early Mathematics:* Graphing birthday dates
Creative Expression/Arts Appreciation: Finding/observing visual patterns

Procedure: In circle time teacher will introduce the topic of learning about the months of the year by telling the children her birthday month as an example. The teacher then will ask what month children were born (if they don't know, the teacher can tell them based on the family/child information for the school). The teacher has prepared a graph of the months with several small magnets to demonstrate the presentation visually and encourages children to put a magnet on their month on the graph. The teacher asks children if they can find any "pattern" to the graph—in this case, a month or months they can see more often—or why no pattern is seen.

Modification: The teacher can use a graph with a corresponding vertical number line and small photos of children. When these are graphed, it will be easy for children to count how many photos are in each column.

Follow-up Activity: In small groups of 4 or 5, the children will look through magazines, newspapers, and ads at their tables and select any pictures, photos, words, and numbers that remind them of their birthday or birthday month. Then they will cut out the selections and glue them on colored paper. Children will tell why they selected specific objects, words, or numbers, and the teacher will make sure that each of their stories is different depending on each child's family and experiences although their birth month may be the same. The class will revisit the chart to connect the birth month and the child's birthday date later and put their artwork on the steppingstone to create a special design for each child. These can be placed in their school/classroom or children can take them home.

USING RHYTHM STICKS

Domain: *Physical Development:* Learning body control; active movement patterns
Creative Expression/Arts Appreciation: Observing oral patterns; gaining listening and singing skills

Figure 4.2. Ways Rhythm Sticks Can Be Used to Keep a "Beat"

1. Gently tap body parts such as knees, head, tummy.
2. On the floor, shuffle them back and forth like a "train" to the beat.
3. In the air, crisscross them and, with the rhythm, "fly a plane" in the sky.
4. Play various "pretend" instruments such as drums or violin.
5. Have the sticks "go for a walk" or a "run" (depending on speed of beat).
6. Use actual "sounds" to match the beat, such as "choo-choo, choo-choo, choo-choo."

Procedure: Using rhythm sticks with preschoolers reinforces several skills in addition to rhythm. The teacher models by making a steady beat with the rhythm sticks in various ways (hitting them together, hitting floor or desk) that can be fun, silly, and playful. It is best to model a steady beat instead of a more complex rhythm pattern for preschoolers because until a child can keep a steady beat, the more complex rhythm pattern will be too difficult. Young children learn rhythm by seeing, hearing, and feeling the beat.

This activity also reinforces listening skills. However, if the younger preschool children don't use the sticks to do just as the teacher does, allow them to explore with the sticks, as long as they are being safe. There are endless ways to use rhythm sticks and older preschoolers can give their own ideas as the activity progresses.

Helping children learn to keep a steady beat gives them the ability to learn more complex rhythm beats as they get older. The brain connections for steady rhythm are most important to nurture before the age of 5. Rhythm sticks can also be used with toddlers, but for younger toddlers, it is especially important to use shorter sticks, such as 8" long instead of the traditional 10–12" sticks. Figure 4.2 gives suggestions on varied ways rhythm sticks can be used.

Modification: For children who need more feedback, drumsticks that make louder noises (e.g., Pocket Stix) provide children who have limited hand strength with enhanced auditory feedback.

OBSERVING AND TOUCHING THE FISH

Domain: *Science:* Learning animal parts; observing differences; practicing scientific exploration
Language Development: Hearing and using new vocabulary

Procedure: This activity requires one large whole fish (or two smaller ones), which should be put in a freezer for at least 3 days to ensure it is very solidly frozen. Before the activity, the teacher will read some books about fish (e.g., "*One Fish, Two Fish*" or a children's science book on fish). Then the fish will be placed in a waterproof dish on the science table, and the teacher will say: "For the next few days we will have a frozen fish (if species is known the actual name can be used: Cod, Salmon), and you are welcome to look at the fish and explore the parts of the fish with gentle touches." The various parts of the fish can be identified, and children can draw pictures of the fish after they have explored its features. It would be best if an adult (perhaps a parent volunteer) could sit at that table and talk to the children about the fish they are exploring. Each day, after about 1 hour of the fish being observed, it should be put back in the freezer. With this care, the fish should be available for exploration for at least a week. Children really are fascinated by this activity, and it allows them to safely observe an animal that they could not observe easily. Because young children learn much through sensory experiences, an actual experience such as this provides a much richer brain connection than reading about fish in a book. This experience gives enactive knowledge, reading about fish gives iconic knowledge, and the name "fish" is symbolic knowledge.

Modification: For children with sensory aversion, gloves can be worn that allow them to experience the fish through touch without the sensation of the texture of the fish.

TREASURE HUNT

Domain: *Social Studies:* Creating a map of an area; using a map to find a specific location
Social/Emotional Development: Working with peers
Science: Solving practical problems

Procedure: Children will be asked to create a map of their classroom or playground area. The teacher will use the map to provide directions (e.g., take three steps from the front of the slide to the right) to lead small groups of children to a previously hidden "treasure." The teacher will assist children in hiding the treasure and in creating directions on their map for another group of children to find.

NAME THAT EMOTION

Domain: *Social/Emotional Development:* Recognizing and accurately labeling feelings about self and others
Language Development: Participating in collaborative conversations
Creative Expression/Arts Appreciation: Expressing different emotions through facial expression and body language

Procedure: Children will take turns standing in front of the group and displaying a selected "emotion" from a deck of emotion face cards (e.g., happy, sad, mad, scared, surprised) while other children try to name the emotion. Once a child guesses the correct emotion, the teacher can lead a discussion on what situations might make someone feel that way and suggest some strategies that we can use when we feel a particular emotion that makes us worried or frightened. The child who guessed the correct emotion will then have a turn and the game will continue.

ANIMALS ON PARADE

Domain: *Physical Development:* Performing a variety of gross motor actions
                  Social/Emotional Development: Perspective taking/imitation

Procedure: The teacher announces that the class will play a game of "follow the leader—animal style." Each child picks a card depicting an animal and has to follow the child selected as "leader" around the playground walking like the animal on the card. When the leader announces "Trade!" the leader moves to the back of the line and all the children give their animal card to the person behind them and adopt the walk of their new animal. The new "leader" then moves around the playground and the game continues. One variation could be to create an obstacle course to make this more challenging or to also require children to make the sounds made by their selected animal.

PLANNING THE PRESCHOOL DAY

Sometimes early childhood educators are so tied to a special schedule that they do not think they can incorporate more varied and challenging activities into their daily educational plan. However, one important aspect of brain development is that having changing activities and social and mental challenges is vital if children are going to have brains with rich neuronal connections. Figure 4.3 contains a sample of a daily plan that shows how the incorporation of interesting and challenging activities can be done during the preschool day.

ENHANCING THE BRAIN DEVELOPMENT OF JESÚS, RUBY, AND BILLY

The preschool age period marks a time of rapid growth in the brain's communication systems and an increased ability for self-regulation. During the preschool years, children demonstrate increased social development and symbolic representation; however, they still require assistance to complete some cognitive tasks, especially ones that are unfamiliar in their home

Figure 4.3. Preschool Day Schedule

7:15–8:00	Arrival / Table Activities
8:00–8:30	Morning Provocations
8:30–9:15	Breakfast Served Family Style
	Music and Movement
9:15–10:15	Outdoor Investigations
	Document bugs found in the garden using cameras, drawings, descriptions, etc.
10:15–10:30	Morning Meeting
	Discussion:
	-how and where to find bugs
	Prepare environment for bugs in classroom:
	-characteristics of insects
	-how insects help us
10:30–11:15	Indoor Investigations
	Explore sensory table of a deconstructed flower; create mandalas with natural materials; nature collages
11:15–11:30	Literacy Circle
	Child choice of book: *Over in the Garden; The Very Hungry Caterpillar; There Was an Old Lady Who Swallowed Some Bugs; The Very Quiet Cricket; Bugs, Bugs, Bugs*
11:30–12:15	Lunch
12:15–2:15	Nap/Rest Time
2:15–2:30	Snack
2:30–4:00	Indoor Investigations
	Parts of plants; herb rubbings; flower press; making flower cards
4:00–5:15	Outdoor Investigations
	Dig in dirt to make a new garden; plant sunflower seeds/look for bugs. Bring magnifying glasses and bug cases.

environments. Thus preschool-age children benefit from exposure to a wide variety of growth-enhancing experiences. The focus of a preschool curriculum should be on play-based activities that provide opportunity to address a variety of developmental domains. Caregivers should include choice within activities to provide children with increased sense of control.

For example, the preschool can provide Jesús with a wide range of different experiences from those he might encounter in his home environment, especially in areas related to language growth and understanding. He will enhance his brain's competence in both his native language and in English if his teachers use both languages, and the language centers of his brain will become more complex.

Although Ruby does not have a language problem, she is hesitant to participate in social and active experiences, either because of shyness or learning constraints in her home environment. Being able to "let go" and use her body actively can result in an expansion of her brain's physical, social, and cognitive pathways as she uses her body in the group setting and follows directions for movement. Many children have constraints in their home environments that do not allow them to use their whole range of physical skills.

Children such as Billy can also make rich brain communication connections through the experiences of the preschool program. By being engaged in interesting activities, Billy will stimulate his brain to work at its highest capacity, resulting in growth in effective functioning. Sometimes children with special needs are not encouraged to have full participation, but ways to adapt activities so they can fully participate are very important.

Also, for Jesús, Ruby, and Billy, their observations of how the other children in the preschool respond to the varied activities can enhance their brain communication growth and give them models of behavior that can foster their brain development. The brain grows through both observation and action.

QUESTIONS FOR DISCUSSION

1. How might you modify one of the above activities for Jesús, in consideration of his language needs? Explain how this modification might enhance his brain development.
2. How might you ensure that Billy is getting meaningful learning from one of the above activities, rather than just "hanging out"? What other adaptations for Billy could be helpful for his brain development?
3. Why does body movement to music seem to be a good entry to participation in group activities for Ruby? Suggest other "entry-type" activities that she could engage in that might enhance her brain development.
4. Think about some of the typical activities that are suggested in curriculum books for preschoolers. Select two of them and analyze them in relation to what brain development activity they provide. If you see an activity that does not seem to be a good facilitator of preschool brain development, explain why it might not be appropriate for a preschool-age child.

SUGGESTIONS FOR FURTHER READING/LISTENING

Bergen, D. (2015). Play as a method of assessing young children's learning and development: Past, present, future. In O. Saracho & B. Spodek (Eds.), *Contemporary perspectives on assessment and evaluation in early childhood education* (pp. 221–246). Charlotte, NC: Information Age.

DiCarlo, C. F., Baumgartner, J. J., Stephens, A., & Pierce, S. H. (2013). Using structured choice to increase child engagement in low-preference centres. *Early Child Development & Care, 183*(1), 109–124.

Lee, L. (2019). When technology met real-life experiences: Science curriculum project with technology for low-income Latino preschoolers. In N. Kucirkova, J. Rowsell, & G. Falloon (Eds.), *International handbook of learning with technology in early childhood theory and method* (pp. 338–348). New York, NY: Routledge.

Lee, L., & Tu, X. (2016). Digital media for low-income preschoolers' effective science learning: A case study of iPads with a social development approach. *Computer in the Schools, 33*(4), 1–14.

Miss Gail and the Jumpin' Jam Band's Active Music, Active Bodies, Active Brains CD is available at http://missgailmusic.com under OUR MUSIC and also on streaming music platforms such as Spotify, Apple, and Amazon Music.

CHAPTER 5

Fostering Brain Development in the Kindergarten/Primary Curriculum

Eden

Eden, age 7, walks around the playground shuffling his feet and looking at the ground. Nearby, several children are engaged in a game of kickball, while a group of girls huddle on the steps, taking turns playing jump rope. Eden usually stays on the periphery of the playground, but he stops to talk to the teacher on duty: "Let me tell you everything I know about Pluto. Pluto is 7.5 billion kilometers from the Earth. It would take 9.5 years to get there. When I got there, I would be almost 18, even though I wouldn't go because Pluto is not really a planet." Mrs. Simmons smiles and offers, "I have heard that . . . " Before she can finish her thought, Eden raises his hand in her face, turns, and walks off. This conversational style predominates in Eden's interaction with others, and it is particularly ill-received by his peers. Mrs. Simmons mentions her encounter with Eden to his classroom teacher; both teachers have been searching for ways to help Eden become more engaged with the other children. They decide to discuss Eden's style of social conversation and lack of peer interaction with the special education teacher to see if that teacher can give them some advice regarding ways to improve Eden's social skills.

Maigret

When Maigret was in preschool and kindergarten, she seemed to be a happy child with good social skills and many ideas for pretend play. She often engaged in elaborate play scenarios with a few other girls and they seemed to be great friends. Now that Maigret is in 2nd grade, however, she acts like a different child because she rarely talks to anyone, seems unable or unwilling to do her class assignments, and is often absent. Her teacher, Mrs. Bland, has tried to contact the family; when she called the cellphone number in her file, a man answered, identified himself as Maigret's father, listened briefly to the teacher, and then said Maigret's mother was not able to come to the phone. Last Monday, the teacher noted that when Maigret came into the classroom, she seemed to be limping and her arms seemed too weak to hang up her coat. Mrs. Bland asked Maigret if she was ill, but the child said "no," although she had a frightened look. During the class activities that day Maigret barely participated, as though the weight of problems on her mind prevented her from concentrating on anything else. The teacher is now wondering if Maigret's family is having some major financial difficulties or if Maigret is encountering some type of neglect or abuse, either from family members or other individuals. She has decided to ask the school counselor to talk to Maigret to find out if there is some action that needs to be taken by school personnel.

Ying

Ying has always been an excellent student, and now that she is in 3rd grade, her academic progress is outstanding. Her teacher, Mr. Bluet, is planning to recommend her for the gifted education group. Since she was 4 years old, Ying has been taking piano lessons and her parents have been very supportive (if not demanding) of her dedicated practice and focus on perfect performance. Although her musical talents seem extraordinary for a child of her age, Ying is also a very sociable child who enjoys playing games (especially computer-generated math games), and her verbal skills are excellent. However, Mr. Bluet has noticed that there are times when Ying has "meltdowns" at school, especially when she is interacting with other children who disagree with her ideas. Because of his concern that Ying could be experiencing "burnout" at this early age, Mr. Bluet did speak to Ying's parents about her strenuous schedule and suggested that they make sure she has time to relax and enjoy "downtime." However, Mr. Bluet does not feel certain that they valued his suggestions.

REVIEW OF BRAIN DEVELOPMENT
AT THE KINDERGARTEN/PRIMARY AGE LEVEL

In planning kindergarten/primary curriculum, it is important to consider how brain development occurs during the kindergarten/primary years. Figure 5.1 gives a review of brain development information at the kindergarten/primary age level.

Figure 5.1. Review of Brain Development at Kindergarten/Primary Age Level

- Although synaptogenesis (creation of neural networks) continues during the 6–8 age period, the process of pruning (cutting back on) neural networks becomes more prominent.
- At about age 7, synaptic density of the frontal lobe of the brain is at its highest.
- The amount of energy (as measured in glucose use) needed for brain functioning gradually declines as the pruning process occurs; children activate larger brain areas than adults when doing cognitive tasks.
- Reaction time speed, memory strategies, problem solving, motor coordination, test performance, metalinguistic awareness, self-efficacy knowledge, and social competence show increases.
- Children can focus more successfully on tasks requiring attention and inhibit impulses.
- Beginning readers have different brain patterns than both preschoolers and older readers.
- The P300 brain wave, related to being conscious of one's own mental experiences, becomes evident during the primary years. It reaches full amplitude and speed in adolescence.
- As changes in brain wave functioning occur at the time Piaget (1952) labeled "concrete operational thought," children begin to reason logically if they have concrete materials to help them do so.
- There are more refinements of brain structures and functions; brains become more individualized and children of this age show particular interests that they intensely explore.
- A more formal learning environment may enable the brain's memory functions to begin to operate more efficiently, as Vygotsky (1978) suggested .
- By age 6, there are individual differences in how children's brains have developed, with phonological awareness, vocabulary, and mathematical abilities differing in individual children.
- Formal music training, which may begin during this age period, may enhance maturity and integration of auditory and motor areas of the brain, as well as enhancing tonal sensitivity.
- Some differences in male and female brains (e.g., hippocampus larger in girls; amygdala larger in boys) may begin to be evident, but how such differences are related to behavior is unclear.
- As societal messages about what may be appropriate behavior for girls and for boys become stronger, gender differentiation of activities may also result in differentiation in some brain development patterns.
- Learning disabilities and attention deficit disorders, which may be related to brain maturation patterns, are often diagnosed in this early elementary time period.

CURRICULUM PRIORITIES AT
KINDERGARTEN/PRIMARY AGE LEVEL

Children of this age level should have gained a wide range of positive past experiences that prepared them for being successful during this initial period of more formal education. However, if some children come from environments that do not encourage their optimum brain development, they may not have as rich a set of synaptic connections as other children in the class. Educators must be knowledgeable about all children's past experiences and varied abilities so that they can assist them to continue to "grow their brains" during the kindergarten/primary years. In each educator's class, the range of child experiences may be quite wide, and thus the children's brain development may be quite varied. For example, although some children have the opportunity to travel to other parts of their country, to be active in a range of settings in their local area (e.g., libraries, museums, zoos, farms, airports), and to have adults who play games with them, read to them, and encourage them to talk about their experiences, other children may have fewer brain-enhancing opportunities.

Many primary schools no longer have separate music programs, and so it is important for teachers to continue to include music experiences in their classroom. Of course, it would be good to have specific music training for teachers (e.g. the Orff method; see Sun, 2017), but teachers can include music experiences even if they are not especially musical themselves. For instance, playing a specific "welcome" song each morning when children arrive is key to helping them feel comfortable. Similarly, playing quiet music at appropriate times, using music or "chants" to aid in cleanup and transitions between activities, employing music to learn specific tasks or academics, and playing a "good-bye" song can help children know what to expect in the day. Having "intentional" music can be invaluable for daily continuity and can give the teacher a greater sense of nondidactic control of the classroom. Teachers should have basic knowledge about the importance of keeping a steady musical beat, matching a musical pitch, and singing in tune. Enthusiasm, joy, and animation can go a very long way toward making music fun and helping create a love for music in children.

Especially important for brain development during this age period are experiences that engage children in the following activities:

1. Appropriate musical experiences (e.g., singing songs pitched high enough for children to sing along, rather than at a pitch comfortable only for the teacher); opportunities to hear unusual instruments/song patterns from various countries; exposure to simple dance patterns, such as clogging, and different rhythms; singing "choir" songs with other children in which the lyrics and musical

patterns are learned (this may or may not lead to a "performance"); and using many simple instruments in the early elementary classroom, such as recorders, ukuleles, xylophones, and "boomwackers"

2. Continued opportunities for "creative time" (e.g., playtime) in which the child can make choices of the art media to use and the topic to paint/draw, including such activities as designing "sets" for plays or engaging in group building of dioramas or other "small worlds"

3. Opportunities to select books for pleasure reading and free reading time at least weekly

4. Teacher engagement in short but regular reading times of "classic" books that are more difficult than grade level (perhaps for 10 minutes a day right after lunch)

5. Motor skill practice opportunities either at recess, in the gym, or in the classroom (young elementary students need "break times")

6. Extended time periods for working with materials that can be used in many different ways (e.g., harder puzzles, Lego or other "table" blocks, clay, paint)

7. Opportunities to create "small world" pretend environments (e.g., diorama of other countries, historical times, or space exploration) that involve miniature houses, cars, buildings, animals, and people and a place in classroom where the small world can remain to be worked on over a period of time

8. An atmosphere that encourages child humor development (e.g. teacher-initiated riddles as well as the teacher being "fooled" by children's riddles and showing enjoyment of other humor attempts by children)

9. Performing "helper" activities in which children do tasks for teachers or other children (e.g., cleanup time, washing tables). Of course, by kindergarten/primary age, there are already standard requirements that must be met for reading, mathematics, science, social studies, art, and music, but these should be designed to engage many brain development areas. They should not just focus on children's paper-and-pencil or computer responses to prepared materials

Brain development during this age level involves pruning of less often used synaptic connections and the strengthening of more often used synaptic connections. Therefore, it is important to provide both a wide range of experiences and opportunities for individual children to become "expert" at certain types of experiences that are of particular interest to them. The goals of brain development during this age period are to support broad child competence and to help children hone individual skills of their own choosing. Thus K–3 teachers should be especially aware of individual children's interests and strengths and give every child the opportunity to strengthen brain synapses in areas of their own special abilities and interests.

Those kindergarten/primary age children who remain in environments that are not encouraging of their healthy brain growth will continue to need special consideration and educators often will need the assistance of special educators and other professionals to assist in providing experiences to enhance their brain development. If children happen to live in a poor environment for brain health (e.g., parental drug use, poverty, food deprivation, abuse), they may continue to need to be exposed to experiences that are less demanding or of different character. Thus it is especially important for kindergarten and primary grade educators to be aware of what experiences may be needed for such children and to continue to provide "hands-on," "real-world," and "playful" activities. This will enable children who may need more support to continue rich brain development and to be successful in the school environment. Although the kindergarten/primary years are ones in which brain pruning does begin, this time period can also be one that continues to encourage greater brain synaptic development by giving all children brain-enriching experiences.

The suggestions given in earlier chapters about the importance of early childhood educators having the correct knowledge about children's brain development and how to foster academic as well as other types of learning with rich "whole brain" interactive experiences is especially important at this time period. The "pseudo-knowledge" about brain enhancement (e.g., "right-brain' or 'left-brain"/ "learning styles") sometimes presented to primary grade educators even in approved workshops or training sessions should be counteracted by their accurate knowledge of the developing brain. Experiences that encourage playfulness, creativity, and self-confidence are important to include in the curriculum as well as required standards.

The following section suggests a sample of curriculum activities that may facilitate kindergarten/primary age brain development. Of course, there are many other activities that also can be relevant for this development. The growth areas addressed use the NAEYC standards labels.

SAMPLE CURRICULUM ACTIVITIES
(CAN BE ADAPTED FOR PRESCHOOLERS)

CHOOSING MY WORK PLAN

Domain: *Early Literacy:* Making lists; reading self-chosen books
Social/Emotional Development: Self-monitoring behavior; managing learning time

Procedure: At least once a week, children should have a "choice day" or "choice afternoon" (perhaps Friday afternoon) in which they can choose which required academic activity (e.g., reading, math, science, social studies, writing, music/art, or other creative activity) they wish to do first, second,

and third during that time period. Each child writes a brief "study plan" for that time period and an "activity plan" for optional choices (e.g., game playing, book reading, science activity) that they can do after the required work is completed satisfactorily that day, and then they follow that plan, with teacher monitoring and assistance if needed.

The teacher's role includes observing how well each child can self-monitor and complete tasks, ask for needed help, and complete the assigned work soon enough to have the time for a self-chosen activity. At first children may have difficulty with this procedure (especially if they have never had an opportunity to plan for themselves). However, after only a few sessions, most children will be very engaged and productive, and the teacher can focus time on those children who seem to need more adult direction in order to develop self-monitoring or self-regulation skills. Because self-monitoring is an especially important brain-related skill, it is very important that children of this age level begin to have short and well-supervised opportunities to learn this skill.

COPY THE RHYTHM GAME

Domain: *Physical Development:* Motor/small muscle beat training
Language Development: Learning "vocables"
Creative Expression/Arts Appreciation: Learning rhythm and sound patterns

Procedure: This game works when children can keep a steady beat and are ready to learn more complex rhythms. The game expands on the activities mentioned in previous chapters for infants and preschoolers who have used shaker eggs, drums, or other types of rhythm instruments. For the game each child should have an instrument such as a drum, pair of sticks, or tambourine. The teacher models a pattern, along with a *vocable*, which is spoken along with the instrument being played. Generally, this would fit into a 4-beat measure or rhythm pattern. This vocable is the teacher's choice. Many teachers choose traditional sounds for the vocable, such as TA for quarter notes and TI for eighth notes.

So the teacher plays her instrument while saying TA TA TI-TI TA, and the children "copy" this pattern, playing and saying the vocable with the teacher. Then the teacher says *freeze*! If the children can repeat this pattern, the teacher does another one for them to try. The patterns can get more complex as they go along in the school year and have mastered the simpler rhythms. For example, other patterns can be demonstrated, such as:

TA TI-TI TI-TI TA

or the teacher can put two 4-beat patterns together, such as:

TA TI-TI TI-TI TA
TI-TI TA TI-TI- TA

The vocable can also become more creative, such as CAT for quarter notes and KIT-TY for eighth notes, giving a pattern such as CAT CAT KIT-TY CAT.After children become familiar with basic patterns and have mastered them, the teacher can let each child take a turn to be the leader. This activity can be very useful during transition times, as it can be shorter or longer, depending on time available.

SHAPE FIND

Domain: *Early Mathematics:* Identifying shapes
Social/Emotional Development: Interacting with peers
Social Studies: Discussing meaning and importance of familiar places

Procedure: Using laminated photographs of familiar local places, challenge children to find shapes within the photographs and draw them onto the picture using an Expo marker. Children can work in pairs to look at the local landmarks and identify and name shapes.

Modification: Children can be provided with a template of shapes to look for and the teacher can support by providing the shape names. The teacher can also provide choices between two shapes and ask the child which shape an object in a picture most closely resembles.

TREE FARM

Domain: *Science:* Caring for living things; using basic vocabulary to name and describe plants
Early Mathematics: Collect data on plant growth; make comparisons between types of plant growth; measure amount of water

Procedure: Using small pots, have children scoop dirt and plant a tree seed so that each child has his own tree. Read a book or discuss with children what is necessary for plants to grow, and incorporate the care of the plants into your daily routine. Introduce mathematical concepts by specifying how much water each plant will need each day and have children measure out the amount of water given. Children can keep a journal with the date and the amount of water given. As the seedlings sprout, children can take measurements of the growth using a ruler and record the data in their journal. Once the seedlings have matured, children can take them home to plant in their yard or they can be planted at school.

FAVORITE CHARACTER VOTE

Domain: *Early Mathematics:* Graphing data
Language Development: Express a preference and justifying it

Procedure: When reading a book, ask children to name their favorite character in the story. Create a laminated graph with Velcro columns for each character. Each child has a square with her name and/or photo on the square. Children can place their square in a column to vote for their favorite character. The teacher can use the graph to summarize class results, using the words "more" and "less" and quantifying results. Children can be asked to determine how many more votes one character got than another by interacting with the squares.

ALTERNATIVE ENDINGS

Domain: *Language Development:* Participating in collaborative conversation; expressing unique ideas
Creative Expression/Arts Appreciation: Drawing favorite alternative ending to stories

Procedure: After reading a book, ask the children what they wished would have happened in the story and ask them to create an alternative ending. Ask children to talk to a friend about their idea, then have the group share.

Write these ideas on a white board and ask guiding questions; allow children to ask questions of each other. After several ideas have been generated, have children draw a picture of their favorite alternative ending.

LEARNING CLASSROOM RULES OR GUIDELINES

Domain: *Social Studies:* Developing understanding of the importance of rules
Language Development: Participating in collaborative conversation with peers and adults
Social/Emotional Development: Demonstrating control over impulsive behaviors
Creative Expression/Arts Appreciation: Drawing a picture or taking a photograph illustrating each classroom rule

Procedure: The teacher will lead a class discussion on "classroom rules" and how rules keep us safe and considerate in the classroom. Children will be asked to contribute ideas on rules that should be included, explaining why their rule is important. (For example, Children might say, "Everyone should be listened to"; "No one should be mean to anyone"; "Everyone should follow fire alarm directions"; and so on.) Then the teacher would ask, "What guidelines do we all need to agree to for this to work?" (Children might say "Don't interrupt"; "Don't yell out"; or "Don't put someone down"; and so on.) Once the rules have been decided, everyone (students and teachers) would sign the list and it would be posted in the room. The children could also draw a picture or take a photograph depicting a rule. Sometimes during the year there might be reminders (by either students or teachers) to check the list if the rules seem to have been forgotten.

PERFORMING CLASSROOM RESPONSIBILITIES

Domain: *Social Studies:* Carrying out specific responsibilities in the classroom
Language Development: Participating in collaborative conversation with peers and adults
Social/Emotional Development: Following rules and routines
Creative Expression/Arts Appreciation: Drawing a picture or taking a photograph illustrating each classroom job

Procedure: The teacher will lead the class in a discussion about our responsibilities within the classroom and the different jobs that need to be performed each day. Children will be asked to contribute ideas and to explain why the job they suggested is important. Children will then discuss what each job entails and how to assign jobs to students. A job chart will be created using child illustrations or photographs to depict each job. Each job will then be assigned, with rotation of jobs during the year.

INSPIRATION ARTWORK

Domain: *Creative Expression/Art Appreciation:* Observing and/or describing what they like and do not like about particular artwork
Science: Mixing available colors to make new colors
Language Development: Incorporating new vocabulary acquired through conversation to describe the inspirational artwork; engaging in collaborative conversation

Procedure: The teacher will bring in a piece of art for children to study, discussing with them elements of the artwork (e.g., texture, use of colors, line, perspective, position of objects included). Children will be invited to consider what they like and do not like about the inspiration artwork and to create their own art, using the elements they find the most appealing (this project may take more than one day). Once children have completed their own artwork, they can present their pieces to the class.

ACT IT OUT

Domain: *Creative Expression/Art Appreciation:* Role-playing characters from a story
Language Development: Incorporating new vocabulary acquired through the story and demonstrating comprehension of story elements
Social/Emotional Development: Collaborating with peers; perspective taking
Technology: Recording performance for viewing

Procedure: After reading a story, the teacher will solicit volunteers to recreate the story through dramatization using costumes or hand puppets. Children can either prerecord the performance and view with the class or record while performing in front of the class (recording allows children to watch the story repeatedly and share with families, which encourages the child to retell the story). Variation could include having children come up with an alternative ending and performing their new ending.

BALL RACE

Domain: *Science:* Using prior knowledge to make predictions about which ball will go down a ramp first; studying what

conditions cause them to go faster or slower
Language Development: Using varied vocabulary to talk
about experimenting with balls of different size, weight, and
texture
Social/Emotional Development: Playing cooperatively with
peers
Early Mathematics: Using a stopwatch to record time and
make comparison between different ball trajectories

Procedure: The teacher will provide children with a variety of different
balls, varying in size, weight, and texture, and a large ramp (e.g., wide wood
plank). The teacher will ask children to make predictions about which ball
will travel the fastest down the ramp. Children can either release multiple
balls at once and see which lands first or can release them one at a time and
use a stopwatch to record the time and write it in a chart. Children will be
prompted to discuss their predictions and why some objects traveled faster
than others.

The Tightrope Walker

Domain: *Physical Development:* Maintaining balance to walk in a
straight line
Social/Emotional Development: Controlling impulses and
waiting for turn
Creative Expression/Arts Appreciation: Using imagination to
create a story

Procedure: The teacher will place a balance beam on the ground (i.e., garden
timber) for children to walk along to practice their balancing skills. To make
this more engaging, the teacher can ask children to use their imagination to
create a story around why someone would be walking on a tightrope and
what they might be walking over. One variation could include challenging
children to walk quickly or to walk backward. Lively or slow music could
be used to challenge children to walk to the pace of the music.

Modification: For children with balancing issues, a chalk line could be used
in place of a balance beam.

Fruit Salad

Domain: *Physical Development:* Using varied utensils
Social/Emotional Development: Expressing preferences; en-
gaging in conversation with peers
Language Development: Incorporating new vocabulary to

talk about taste
Early Mathematics: Counting objects; making comparisons

Procedure: Children will make their own fruit salad by selecting and preparing fruit. Each child will have their own bowl, cutting board, and utensils to cut fruit. The teacher will begin by asking children if they know the names of each fruit. As each fruit is introduced, the teacher will give children a taste. Once all fruit has been introduced, children are free to request what they would like; requesting some fruit, such as blueberries or blackberries, by quantity (i.e., "I would like 5 blueberries") and/or indicating when they would like "more." Children will practice bilateral coordination by stabilizing fruit with one hand, while using a knife to cut with the other hand. Once children have cut all of their fruit, they will cut a piece of citrus of their choice, squeeze it onto their salad, toss, and eat.

What's in the Clouds?

Domain: *Creative Expression/Art Appreciation:* Creating a work of art that was seen in the clouds
Language Development: Using descriptive vocabulary and imagination to express ideas
Social/Emotional Development: Engaging in reciprocal conversation with peers

Procedure: Teachers take children outside on a sunny day when there are clouds in the sky to lay in the grass and use their imagination to see what they find in the clouds. Children can draw what they see and create stories about their cloud characters to share with others. They can take their stories and turn them into a book for the classroom library.

Creating Interactive Song Extensions

Domain: *Language Development:* Expanding vocabulary
Creative Expression/Arts Appreciation: Expanding music understanding
Social/Emotional Development: Following ideas of other children; taking turns

Procedure: Many of the songs used in preschool can be included and expanded to be more complex and interactive for kindergarten/primary-age children. Any familiar songs can be used in this activity as long as a "funny" substitution can be suggested by the children. It is important to accept almost any idea from the children (unless it is socially inappropriate) even if the suggestion is silly or repetitive; the teacher should encourage children to think that all their ideas can be creative and good. Here are two examples of songs that can be extended in this way:

> "Muffin Man": Do you know the *muffin* man, / The *muffin* man, the *muffin* man, /
> Do you know the *muffin* man, / Who lives *on Drury Lane*?
> Children think of a food they like and where the "man" lives. For example: "Do you know the *pizza man*? He lives on *Pepperoni Lane*."
>
> "Down by the Bay": Down by the bay where the watermelons grow/ Back to my home I dare not go / For if I do, my mother will say:/ "Have you ever seen a *DUCK driving a truck*, down by the bay?" Children can think of different kinds of animals, and either teacher or children can come up with the funny action part. For example: (First child:) *Have you ever seen a SNAKE* . . . (Second child:) *baking a cake?*

RHYTHM AND TEMPO GAME

Domain: *Physical Development:* Learning to control gross and fine motor movements
Language Development: Expanding listening skills for tempos
Creative Expression/Arts Appreciation: Experiencing body rhythm changes and gaining artistic awareness

Procedure: The children in the class stand so that they are not touching anyone or anything. They then choose a pose as if they were a statue and they cannot move until they hear the drum sound. Initially the teacher has the drum, but later children might lead. As the children listen to the beat of the drum they can only move once for every beat, but at each beat they should move one part of their body. They cannot touch anyone in the room during this activity and must not be moving when the drum is not playing. As the tempo of the drum changes, speeding up and slowing down, the children match the speed of their movements to the tempo of the drum.

A BOOMWHACKER ORCHESTRA

Domain: *Physical Development:* Extending physical skill in music making
Language Development: Expanding listening skills for tempos
Creative Expression/Arts Appreciation: Gaining new ways of music expression

Procedure: Boomwhackers are among the simplest of instruments. A boom-whacker is a lightweight, hollow tube made of plastic that has been tuned to a specific musical pitch by using different lengths. They are color-coded as to tone. Boomwhackers are considered part of the percussion family because they are played by hitting them on the ground, leg, or table, and a specific pitch is made depending on the length of the boomwhacker used. Boomwhackers are most commonly used in elementary music classrooms as an inexpensive alternative or supplement to traditional pitched instruments such as xylophones. One of the most popular ways to use them is by giving each child or group of children boomwhackers with specific pitches. A song is made by collaboratively "playing" them at a specific point in the song in order to make a melody. They also can be used as a fun way to reinforce rhythm, as a "call and response" activity, or to teach children about chord progressions. There are many online color-coded resources and programs available if a teacher is interested in incorporating boomwhackers into the classroom. (See Schulkind, 2015.)

LEARNING TO PLAY AN INSTRUMENT

Domain: *Physical Development:* Refinement of small motor skills
                    Language Development: Learning names of chords
                    Creative Expression/Arts Appreciation: Understanding the process of music creation

Procedure: Once children have obtained basic musical competence (keeping a steady beat and matching a pitch/singing in tune), children of this age level can begin to learn to play a basic instrument, such as the ukulele. Because of its size and low-cost alternatives, as well as the fact that there are only four strings and they are relatively easy to press down, the ukulele is a much better early instrument option than a guitar. There are many songs that can be played on the ukulele if children know only two or three chords. However, since children develop differently and do not all have the same attention span, teaching a "real instrument" such as a ukulele works better with some children than others.

To be successful learning an instrument, children need to have a basic knowledge of right and left because all instrument instruction differentiates right and left. When they are young, it doesn't matter if they hit a drum or shake an egg with either hand, but a ukulele is held so that the left hand does the chord fingering, with specific fingers pressing down on specific strings, and the right hand strums. When playing a piano, the right hand plays notes in the treble clef and the left hand generally plays notes written in the bass clef. Recorder fingering requires hands to be in a specific position to cover the proper holes to make a note. Even drums require the right and left hands to do different things. Rhythm, pitch, and more intense instrument instruction should be limited to about 10-minute intervals. This activity may be one that the school music teacher can use if the classroom teacher does not have instrument-playing capabilities. Other instruments well-suited as initial options for learning musical skills are xylophones and harmonicas. Simple tunes can be learned by children of this age with any of these instruments. Drums also can be used to teach more elaborate rhythm patterns.

PLANNING THE KINDERGARTEN/PRIMARY DAY

Depending on the particular school district, the curriculum may be closely prescribed or it may be more general; in the latter case, educators have more decision-making power over specific learning activities to use to meet curricular goals. In a curriculum that prescribes what learning activities must occur on a daily basis, educators may have to work harder and more creatively to meet the learning needs of the wide range of children in the class. However, one very important aspect of brain development is that all children should have a range of activities (not just paper-and-pencil or computer-program ones). They also need a range of social, physical, and mental challenges in order to develop brains with strong, rich, and active neuronal connections. Every teacher should have the opportunity to plan one or two activities a week that engage children in physically and mentally active playful "work."

Figure 5.2 contains sample daily plans for a kindergarten day and a Grade 3 day that show how the incorporation of challenging activities can be done for children at these grade levels.

ENHANCING THE BRAIN DEVELOPMENT OF
EDEN, MAIGRET, AND YING

Often educators begin to work with children of this age similarly to the way that they would engage with children who are older. That is, they may think that the brain's conceptual and emotional activity is already fully developed and thus may believe that a teaching style involving static learning, presenting material orally, and requiring a long attentional focus are appropriate for children of the K–3 age range. However, the brain development of children this age is not yet the same as that of the adult brain, the adolescent brain, or even the preadolescent brain. For example, this period of brain development involves the pruning of synaptic density by loss of synapses used rarely and strengthening of synaptic connections that are most used (and hopefully, most useful) for learning. Also, the ability to be fully conscious

Figure 5.2. Sample Kindergarten and Grade 3 Day Schedules

Kindergarten

8:30–9:00	Arrivals, Greetings, and Center Play/ Morning Activities
9:00–9:40	Circle Time with Meditation, Daily Sharing, and Discussion
9:40–10:30	Language Arts with Play Center Activities and Small-Group Instructions
10:30–10:45	Movement with Music
10:45–11:35	Math with Sensorimotor Activities and Small-Group Instructions
11:35–12:15	Lunch and Outdoor/Gym Play
12:15–12:35	Quiet Time Started with Afternoon Meditation (individual reading)
12:35–1:20	Inquiry with Social Studies/Science (or special)
1:20–2:00	Play to Learn (children's choice time or play/learning center including a technology station) or special
2:00–2:20	Snack
2:20–2:45	Afternoon Circle Time (reflection of the day)
2:45–3:00	Closing the Day (cleanup, packing, getting ready for departure)
3:00	Dismissal

3rd Grade

8:30–9:00	Arrivals, Greetings, and Morning Activities/Center Time
9:00–9:20	Morning Circle Time with Meditation, Daily Sharing, and Discussion
9:20–10:00	Language Arts (including small-group activities)
10:00–10:50	Specials/Center Play
10:50–11:50	Math with Inquiry Approaches (including small-group activities)
11:50–12:25	Lunch and Outdoor/Gym Recess
12:25–12:50	Quiet Time Started with Afternoon Meditation (individual reading)
12:50–1:20	Small-Group Activity (language arts/math)
1:20–2:10	Inquiry with Social Studies/Science (or special)
2:10–2:45	Play to Learn (children's choice time or play/learning center including a technology station)
2:45–3:00	Closing the Day (cleanup, packing, getting ready for departure)
3:00	Dismissal

of one's learning experiences develops as the children's P300 brain wave, which is associated with the engagement of attention and discriminating stimuli, becomes more active (this is not completed until adolescence). For optimum brain development, children of this age are still in need of many physically active, sensory interesting, and cognitively supported learning activities.

It is important for teachers to remember that parents of K–3-age children may not be knowledgeable about the brain development that is still occurring during this age level. Teachers can work directly with parents to help them understand how their actions can foster their children's brain development during these years. Eden, Maigret, and Ying will benefit from both parent and teacher attention to following recommendations.

Eden: Eden's lack of social skills has prevented him from having meaningful interactions with children in his grade. His interactions with adults are limited and tend to be one-sided. Teachers should consider social skills training using strategies such as social stories and role play. For a child who has difficulty reading social cues, social stories would center on scripting out a social interaction and providing suggestions for how he could interact with his peers. For instance, reading a social story about interaction on the playground immediately prior to going outside, paired with the use of teacher prompting, could assist Eden in interacting with peers. Additionally, games with rules that involve turn taking would put Eden in conversation with others where he could be taught the rules of the games.

Maigret. If the teacher has noticed major changes in Maigret's behavior and appearance and how her interest, her behavior, and her effectiveness in learning seem to be diminished, it is definitely time for the teacher to begin a process of evaluating why such changes have occurred. She should record some of her observations of Maigret's recent behaviors at school so she can document these changes. Next, the teacher should contact the school counselor, nurse, and other relevant personnel so that they can determine if further investigation of Maigret's home situation or recent life events is warranted. Often a child's changed behavior at school is an indicator of more serious problems in the child's life and these should be investigated and remedied, if possible. Thus teachers may have to make decisions about what steps need to be taken, depending upon the severity of a problem. The teacher might start by contacting the parent to set up a meeting to see how they can work together to help the child, but educators may need to take more serious action if the situation does not improve.

Ying. When a child seems to be progressing very well, it is sometimes the case that parents (or other adults) are so pleased with the child's growing abilities that they make further demands for excellence or expect further new achievements. Although Ying has many abilities and talents, her brain development is still in progress, and, while her learning, musical, and other activities can be brain enhancing, the brain areas involved in emotional and social development are also important. When children signal through behavior or language that they are feeling stressed, adults should evaluate the level of pressure they may be putting on those children and also note how much pressure the children may be putting on themselves. Such children should be encouraged to spend some of their time in less demanding activities or less structured ones, like being able just to "do nothing" some of the time. Often being in the outdoors (walking in natural environments or parks, swimming or bike riding, playing active games, or even just sitting at a backyard picnic) can provide the child's brain with relief from the stress they may be encountering and this will renew their interest and ability to focus on challenging activities at another time.

QUESTIONS FOR DISCUSSION

---

1. What might Eden's teacher include in a social story about interaction on the playground?
2. How could the teacher and parents incorporate the social story into Eden's everyday routine?
3. What type of support does Maigret's teacher need from other school personnel in order to investigate why she has had these behavior changes?
4. Could some training of school personnel in knowing how to deal with potential environmental problems that a child may be facing be added?
5. What type of informational program could be designed for parents of children with gifted abilities like Ying that would help them learn how to provide the appropriate level of support and encouragement for fostering their children's talents?
6. What policies could the school put in place that would enable children to have outdoor time and other less pressure-filled time during the school day?

SUGGESTIONS FOR FURTHER READING

Beach, D., & DiCarlo, C. F. (2016). Can I play, again? Using a literacy ipad app to increase letter recognition & phonemic awareness. *Journal of Teacher Action Research, 2*(2), 70–76.

Beardsley, G., & Harnett, P. (2013). *Exploring play in the primary classroom.* London, United Kingdom: David Fulton.

Bergen, D. (2013). Does pretend play matter? Searching for evidence: Comment on Lillard et al. *Psychological Bulletin, 139*(1), 45–48. doi:10.1037/a0030246

Lee, L. (2016, Summer). A learning journey with Latino immigrant children: An American low-income preschool enhancement project. *Childhood Explorer, 3.* Retrieved from www.childhoodexplorer.org/lipe-project

Reynolds, E., Stagnitti, K., & Kidd, E. (2011). Play, language and social skills of children attending a play-based curriculum school and a traditionally structured classroom curriculum school in low socioeconomic areas. *Australasian Journal of Early Childhood, 36*(4), 120–130.

CHAPTER 6

Fostering Brain Development with Technology-Augmented Materials

---

Nancy

Nancy was a healthy full-term baby and her parents, Jim and Sandy, have been eager to give her every opportunity to develop well. The parents have read about potential developmental dangers that might be connected to children's very early technology use, and so they have decided that their baby will not have an automatic swing or other technology-generated movement devices, watch images on their phones (even though they have noted that when she is upset those images quiet her almost immediately), or interact with Nancy's far-away grandparents' images on a technology-related face-to-face device. She is now 7 months old, and they are noticing that Nancy seems to need more and more attention and is becoming very active within their home environment. They think she will probably crawl soon and maybe even walk very early. This means that her parents must spend more time comforting her when she is fussy, engaging with her in face-to-face interactions, monitoring her increasing movement initiatives, and taking time to make driving visits to see their relatives. Some of their friends think Jim and Sandy are being overly protective and this is limiting their own activities, since their friends have found they can quickly change diapers or even eat out at a restaurant without having their baby be fussy because their phone can easily quiet her, know that the automatic swing keeps her satisfied for a long time period, and believe their own parents really like being able to interact with the baby's image on their computer. Jim and Sandy have busy lives, and they are wondering if using the technology-related devices as "babysitters" is really going to harm Nancy or not. It would make parenting easier if their child could be managed better with the use of these technology-enhanced devices. Since they will be starting Nancy in an early childhood care program soon, they plan to ask the program director about appropriate infant involvement with technology-augmented devices.

Jason and Edwin

Jason and Edwin are 5-year-old boys in the same classroom of a preschool. They love playing at the dramatic play center and the block area, but one of the centers they like the most is the iPad station. One fall day, Jason and Edwin shared their ideas about the seasons when playing an iPad app game about the four seasons. When Jason looked at the trees of fall in the game, he said to Edwin and a teacher, "This is spring! So I am going to do . . . Uh-oh. This is not spring . . . (looking puzzled)." Then Edwin asked, "Hey, why do you think it is spring?" Jason answered, "'Cause it [a tree leaf] has a color here [pointing out the tree of the iPad game]. I was born in spring!" The teacher asked what other colors he often saw on the tree leaves of the iPad game. Then these two boys collaborated on their ideas to build the concepts of the seasons—in particular, spring and fall.

> *Jason:* Yellow . . . and brown . . . ?
> *Edwin:* Yeah! [pointing to a specific part of the tree leaves on the iPad] This is really brown.
> *Jason:* What colors do the tree leaves have in the spring then? Green . . . ?
> *Edwin:* Yeah!
> *Teacher:* Then, how can you decide if this picture [in the iPad app] is spring or fall? How are these two pictures [in the iPad app] different other than colors?
> *Jason:* This has . . . a lot of leaves and this [the other one] doesn't.
> *Edwin:* And that one has the leaves on the ground . . . like the pine trees in my house yard! But they look different.
> *Jason:* Pine tree? Our school has many of those, too. Do they have brown leaves? We should find out!

They went to the window area in the classroom with the iPad to look at the pine trees the school had, and then their conversation continued.

> *Edwin:* No . . . they don't have brown leaves . . . but they have brown leaves on the ground! Did you see those??
> *Jason:* Then . . . Edwin, look at another picture [on the iPad game]. It doesn't have the leaves on the ground. And, it doesn't have many leaves on the tree sticks, here [touching the tree on the iPad].
> *Edwin:* Yeah! But that is not a pine tree. They look different. It looks like [looks out window] that tree [pointing out another tree on the school grounds]! That doesn't have many leaves on the tree sticks!
> *Teacher:* Yes. They are called "branches."
> *Edwin:* Then . . . this one [in the iPad app] is the fall!
> They came back to the station with the iPad and continued to talk about the trees in each season. They wondered why the trees

started to "loose leaves" in the fall and why, in winter, the pine trees still have "leaves." They decided to search more about their questions as a project with the teacher.

Derick

Derick, a 7-year-old diagnosed with Attention Deficit Hyperactivity Disorder (ADHD), has always struggled with working independently. In Mr. Santo's 2nd-grade classroom, his teacher's challenge was rotating his attention back to Derick during independent work time in order to keep Derick engaged in math practice. Mr. Santo's usual practice was to introduce new concepts to children in a whole group, then provide practice activities for children to work independently or in small groups, usually using manipulatives. The problem was that as other children were working, Derick would get off task, needing Mr. Santo's feedback to keep moving. Mr. Santo had recently been investigating applications (apps) that could be used on mobile technology devices, such as an iPad. He had previously used a crowdsourcing platform to raise funds to purchase several iPads for his classroom and reviewed several apps that addressed math concepts for 2nd-grade age level. The benefit of the apps that focus on skill development are that the app itself provides immediate student feedback in the form of visual and audio reinforcement for correct responding, as well as error correction for incorrect responding. According to Mr. Santo, "Since implementing the use of the math app, Derick is much more focused and engaged during independent work. I do not have to stay with him to make sure he is working. The app also provides summarizing feedback so I can tell how many problems he completed correctly."

TYPES OF TECHNOLOGY-AUGMENTED DEVICES FOR CHILDREN

Presently there are three major types of technology-augmented devices affecting children.

1. Child-operated play and communication devices (e.g., tablet-based types, technology-augmented toys, computer software programs)
2. Devices that adults use for safety or to control child actions (e.g., automated swings and mobiles, rocking devices (contain/restrict movement to protect them when necessary).
3. Alternative communication/adaptive technology devices (e.g., positioning equipment, curved spoons, suction bowls , enhanced/assisting devices for movement, hearing, sight, senses, or other abilities). Because there are a variety of technological tools that can assist

young children with disabilities in interacting and accessing their environment, educators should be knowledgeable about these options. For further discussion of such devices, see DiCarlo & Banajee (2000) or DiCarlo, Stricklin, Banajee, and Reid (2001). Figure 6.1 describes these technology-augmented tools.

REVIEW OF POTENTIAL EFFECTS OF TECHNOLOGY-AUGMENTED ACTIVITIES ON BRAIN DEVELOPMENT

Because optimum brain development during the infant through Grade 3 years is so important for long-term success in life, caregivers and educators must be knowledgeable about the most appropriate ways to engage children of these ages in the use of technology-augmented devices. When deciding how much time should be spent on such devices, parents, caregivers, and teachers should consider different factors for different age groups.

Infant/Toddler Age Level

- Infants and very young children should have minimal involvement with technology-augmented devices because they need to focus on "enactive" knowledge development (Bruner, 1964), which involves physical actions on objects and with people in their environment. If too much time is spent engaging in technology-augmented devices without sufficient interaction with humans, young children's bodily engagement and learning as well as cognitive development about their physical world may be impaired. As a result, the American Academy of Pediatrics (AAP) strongly recommends focusing on "creative, unplugged playtime" for infants and toddlers and watching only high-quality programming and coviewing for children aged 18 months to 2 years (AAP, 2018).
- Because this early time period is when "shared intentionality" is developed (Tomasello & Carpenter, 2007), and this essential human quality is learned through interactions with other humans, infants and toddlers need many opportunities to have "in-person" interactions with parents, relatives, caregivers, and other humans. The ability to understand and share the thoughts and intentions of others (i.e., shared intentionality) is an essential human quality that leads to "cognitive intentionality" and to "theory of mind" (knowing other's ideas and thoughts may differ from one's own). At present we do not really understand how this quality in relation to social skills and interactions may or may not be learned from technology-augmented devices (Bergen, 2018).
- Face-to-face human interactions also lead to self-regulation of emotions and behaviors and to the ability to understand and conform to societal

Figure 6.1. Technology for Children with Special Needs

1. *Assistive technology* refers to any piece of equipment or device that is designed to increase or improve the functional ability of an individual with a disability. Examples of assistive technology for young children might include positioning equipment, such as a wheelchair, adapted chair, standing frame, or floor sitter. For young children with physical disabilities, it is important for children to be securely positioned in order for the child to have maximum use of their hands. Being on the same visual field as their peers is also important for social interaction.

2. *Adaptive technology* refers to any modification to a material that assists an individual with a disability in performing an action. Common examples of adaptive technology for young children might include modifications to help young children play more independently, such as placing indoor/outdoor carpet on tray surfaces and rough Velcro on bottoms of toys to help them stay in place or a suction bowl and curved spoon to help children eat more independently.

3. *Augmentative/Alternative Communication systems* supports communication by providing additional means for expressive language. Communication can be unaided (i.e., not needing additional equipment), such as the use of sign language, or aided (i.e., using a technological device), such as the use of a voice output device. Aided technological communication can be low tech, such as using a picture exchange system, or higher tech, such as using a more complex speech-generating device (SGD). When children have difficulty communicating, this can lead to problem behaviors. Problem behaviors can be viewed as children's way of getting their needs met. When caregivers work with young children using augmentative/alternative communication methods, problem behavior is often reduced.

norms. It is presently unknown to what extent extensive early exposure to technology-augmented devices influences young children's ability to gain self-regulation and behavioral engagement.

- If exposure to such devices is used occasionally as a calming technique (or to give parents and other caregivers a short break time), the devices should be safe and either easily manipulated by the child or with time reminders for devices manipulated by adults. The time period of use should be of short duration, and the use should truly be occasional and not routine.

Preschool Age Level

- Time limits should be made in consideration of guidelines from the American Association of Pediatrics, which recommends a maximum of 1 hour of screen time per day for preschoolers (ages 2 to 5) (AAP, 2018, para. 9).
- Adults should check each iPad app's stated learning goals and developmentally appropriate levels to be sure they are actually appropriate.

- Technology software and application should be selected based on skill development using a tool, such as app evaluation criteria for preschoolers (Walker, 2011).
- Teachers should set up a list of the classroom rules for children to follow as a learning community when they use all technology and digital devices.
- Adults should be with them when they are playing. Don't just let them play alone on a regular basis when they play with technology-augmented materials. Monitor, ask, and answer questions that scaffold their learning.
- Teachers should assign a tool such as an iPad for two or more children to play together. Observe what they know, when they are frustrated, and how they collaborate to solve problems and challenge each other.

Kindergarten/Primary Age Level

- Like those for preschoolers, technology software and application should be selected based on skill development using a tool, such as an app evaluation rubric (Burden & Kearney, 2017).
- Consideration should be given to the duration of feedback given by the technological device, as a longer duration of feedback may reduce child responding time (DiCarlo, Schepis, & Flynn, 2009).
- Use an iPad camera, drawing apps, or video/voice recorder as a tool for children to express their learning, ideas, and creative work.
- Technology use should be part of a balanced schedule that includes whole-group and small-group sessions, as well as independent work, as screen time does not lend itself to "dual audiences" (AAP, 2018, p. 2).

- Technology use should be part of an integrated curriculum where other opportunities exist to reinforce the targeted skills as there is recognition that children need "hands-on, unstructured, and social play to build language, cognitive, and social–emotional skills" (AAP, 2018, p.3).

CURRICULUM PRIORITIES FOR TECHNOLOGY-AUGMENTED ACTIVITIES

Teachers should be aware that the uses of technology experiences vary significantly depending on children's ages, socioeconomic status (SES), racial and ethnic groups, and sociocultural contexts (e.g., see Council on Communications and Media, 2016a; Rideout & Hamel, 2006). For instance, high-SES schools invest more in technology support, instructions, and staff while low-SES schools have less technology support in general, and personnel in these schools also frequently demonstrate less confidence in using technology (Melhuish & Falloon, 2010; Warschauer, Knobel, & Stone, 2004). Taking these variations of children's technology uses into consideration, there are many ways that early childhood teachers can develop technology-enhanced curriculum activities.

SAMPLE CURRICULUM ACTIVITIES FOR CHILDREN (MAY BE MODIFIED FOR OTHER AGE LEVELS)

Preschool Age Level

DIGITAL DISPLAY

Domain: *Physical Development:* Finger coloring; coordination with technology device
Social/Emotional Development: Understanding themselves through reflections; recognizing differences between themselves and others
Technology: Creating media stories
Creative Expression/Arts Appreciation: Color shade comparisons and sensitivity; size and placement experience

Procedure: Preschool children's cognitive development can be enhanced by learning various types of images that show differences. When a teacher goes out with children to look at trees and leaves in fall, he can encourage children to collect leaves with a variety of shapes and/or colors (each child should have a paper bag to collect). After collecting the leaves, the teacher can create and display images of children's leaves with a computer or an iPad. Then children can look at the images together to identify differences and similarities, define various colors and shapes, discuss the scents and the feeling they had with the leaves, and draw and paint the leaves on a piece of paper individually or together. The teacher can project these digital images onto a large easel or on the wall set up with paper and paints (teachers can consult a Reggio Emilia–inspired book (e.g., Edwards, Gandini, & Forman, 1998) or online source for guidance on such an approach).

DIGITAL LEARNING GAMES

Domain: *Social and Emotional Development:* Gaining independent
                thinking skills
                Technology: Learning to use appropriate educational apps

Procedures: A classroom can provide developmentally and culturally appropriate educational apps for children's learning. As previously mentioned, there are some rubrics or criteria to evaluate apps for young children. After this evaluation process, a teacher can select apps that are relevant to content or themes children learn in class; the apps can then be placed in a learning center. When presenting these, the teacher should make sure that the digital learning games are presented in tandem with traditional, hands-on learning materials, such as books, artifacts, paper, pencils, crayons, and markers. In this way, children can learn content and build experience with multiple learning modes.

USING SOCIAL SKILLS WITH STEM LEARNING

Domain: *Technology:* Developing iPad skills
                Social/Emotional Development: Interacting with others for
                skill learning
                Early Mathematics and Science: Through use of iPad apps for
                learning

Procedure. The teacher will use learning center times or free playtimes to introduce a learning center station for iPad game play. The iPad apps should be selected to help meet the teacher's learning goals for children's brain development and other learning domains. The apps suggested should be evaluated and selected based on an adoption of the major criteria suggested by experts. For example, one type of app can focus on enhancing children's understanding of math number line concepts and another on science concepts of the seasons (including weather), senses, living/nonliving, and plants/planting. Different apps for various learning goals can be used to accommodate the children's different learning and mastery levels. (See Figure 6.2, which shows a checklist for the uses of technology and interactive media with young children.)

Before starting the actual project with the iPad, the teacher will talk about this activity in a whole-class setting with other adults present (e.g., assistant teacher, student assistant, parent, grandparent). Right before the children's learning center time or free play time, the teacher explains how we use the iPad and the rules that we should have for iPad uses (e.g., each person will take a turn; when a child's name is called then she will use the iPad; each person will have the same amount of time to use per week, and so on). The adult models how to use it step-by-step for 10–15 minutes. Then during the learning/play center time at the "iPad Play Station," the children will play with and explore the iPad. Ideally, this station should have 2 iPads with one of the identified adults to supervise. (This is a great way to involve student assistants or family members in the preschool activity time.) When children have questions or are confused about procedures, the adult supports them by answering or modeling again. This first step includes how to turn on and turn volume up and down on the iPad, and how to open an app. This time is very important as it allows children to be aware of what is going to happen with the teacher and the other adults in the classroom, and what they would use for their learning. In addition, they learn the techniques and functionalities for the effective use of an iPad without any pressure.

After the introduction stage, the teacher uses one or two major apps to facilitate children's learning and prepares other apps for those who may finish tasks early, who need to learn specific concepts with more application, or need to go back to check their previous level of learning. The important thing for the teacher to remember is that when a child has individual iPad instruction time, the child should always be with a "Most Knowledgeable Other (MKO)," which Vygotsky (1978) recommended. When a child starts a game, the teacher or any adult mentioned above, as the MKO, observes how the child solves the problems of the game, checks what strategies the child uses, and reads body cues that may show a child's lack of understanding, confusion, or hesitance. If any child has a question, the adult calmly clarifies the process. If the child does not understand and therefore gets a question wrong, the adult encourages them to play the game again with adult assistance until the child has fully grasped the concept embedded in the game. This process is an illustration of "scaffolding" learning, which is another way to bring children's understanding from the enactive level to the iconic and symbolic levels.

Modification: For children who have difficulty isolating a finger to use a touch screen, a stylus pen can be used.

Kindergarten–Grade 1 Age Level

Digital Stories

Domain: *Language Development:* Using a wide variety of language in creating stories
Social and Emotional Development: Gaining meaning about their life experiences
Technology: Using media to tell stories

Procedure: School-age children can write a collaborative story via digital media. When a teacher decides to read a book, teach a topic, or create a special project with children, she can set up a digital station for drawing and writing about the book, the topic, or the project. There are several apps, such as Book Creator for iPad, Tell About This, Sago Mini Doodlecast, and Little Writer, with which children see pictures and write stories on the iPad. Some apps have a recording function as well. By developing their emergent writing, children can have ample opportunities for digital meaning-making based on their own interpretation, experience, and creativity.

This activity encourages children to work together by building their stories with peers. In addition, the teacher can observe what they discuss, what peer dynamics and relations they have, what problems they encounter, and how they solve them. Once they create stories, the teacher sends the stories to their parents or the children present each story in class to share with their families and peers. If she wants to have more public responses on them, the teacher can post on social media after getting parental permission.

Grades 1–3 Age Level

CREATING CARTOONS

Domain: *Social Studies:* Knowledge application of history, geography, economics
Science: Knowledge application of science
Social and Emotional Development: Collaboration skills
Creative Expression/Arts Appreciation: Adapting art to technology

Procedure. A 3rd-grade classroom can create social studies or science content stories with cartoon apps such as Moodboard Lite, Toontastic, and Comic Maker HD. The students can easily get a variety of photos and cartoons to develop their own ideas to apply what they learn in class into a fun comic/photo strip. This type of tool can be effective and creative for the classroom because it is easy and simple enough to use, search, and modify so that young children can "publish" their own unique story in a fun way. Stories can even be printed from some of those sites.

PLANNING THE TECHNOLOGY-AUGMENTED ENVIRONMENT

The discussions about how exactly technology affects young children's brain are still ongoing. However, there have been serious concerns and warnings from early childhood professionals and pediatricians on excessive technology uses during early childhood years. However, it is necessary for young children to have appropriate experiences with technology and media that encourage them to control the medium and the outcome of the experience, to explore the functionality of these tools, and pretend how they might be used in real life (NAEYC & Fred Rogers Center, 2012). The appropriate experiences for young children and their brain development can be decided by how the particular technologies support each child's learning level, exploration, and curiosity, as well as how such tools contribute to their dialogues and interactions with peers, teachers, and parents. Importantly, decisions about how long they use such devices each day must also be made and monitored.

Therefore, teachers and caregivers should provide enough time for children to explore a technology tool (Lee, 2019) before having set lessons using it. Before children's iPad use, for instance, teachers can allocate instructional time in a whole-class setting. During this time, teachers can explain what to do with the iPad by modeling step-by-step use for 10–15 minutes. This first step includes how to turn on and turn the volume up and down on the iPad, and how to open an app. This "exploratory" time is very important as it allows children to be aware of what and how they will use these technologies for increasing their learning (Lee, 2019). Then the teacher can discuss the rules for iPad use during a classroom discussions (e.g., each person will take a turn; when the classroom teacher or other adult directs, the child will have the iPad use; each child will have the same amount of time to use the device per week; and so on). The teacher can create a learning center where the children can actually play with and explore the iPad. When children have questions or seem confused, the adult should support them by answering or modeling again. Young children are capable of being creative in using technologies when they have relevant and proper adult guidance and involvement. Figure 6.2 shows a checklist for the appropriate uses of technology and interactive media for young children.

ADAPTING TECHNOLOGY-AUGMENTED MATERIALS FOR NANCY, JASON AND EDWIN, AND DERICK

Nancy. Although smartphones and technologically augmented toys are pervasive in present society, they should not be the primary interaction mode experienced by infants and very young children. Parents and other caregivers often find it tempting to quiet a screaming baby with phone images, control infant wiggling when diapering with such devices, and place infants in automatic swings, rockers, and other equipment for long periods of time. However, it is imperative that Nancy and other very young children receive responsive human interaction during this very important early brain development period. Therefore, technology-augmented devices should not

Figure 6.2. Checklist for Effective Uses of Digital Media and Interactive Technology for Early Learning

Criteria	Yes	No	Notes
1. Selection			
Is this digital technology or interactive media age/developmentally appropriate?			
Is this free from violent content and gender/race bias?			
Does this represent various groups of children?			
Can all children in your classroom (including special needs children and ELL students) use this?			
Do young children easily operate and control this, and does your school support this?			
2. Teaching and Learning			
Is this used for individual, small-group, and/or whole-group settings?			
Does this relate to what you teach in class? Can you adequately relate what they learn from this to your teaching?			
Does this effectively connect to school/state/national standards you use?			
Is children's learning meaningfully assessed through this?			
Can you easily collect what children learn with this for the documentation of children's growth?			
Does it enhance family–school relationships and communication?			

Sources: Hillman & Marshall (2009); NAEYC & Fred Rogers Center for Early Learning and Children's Media (2012); Robb et al. (2013)

be used with infants and should be extremely limited for children under 2 years of age. Parents and other caregivers are teaching very young children how to be "human" during this age period and how to respond appropriately to the real world. They must gain enactive cognitive (Bruner, 1964), which involves touching, moving, and experimenting with real objects and people. Thus they should spend the greater proportion of their time in human and real-world interactions rather than in technology-augmented interactions.

Jason and Edwin. Jason and Edwin developed their own ways of using technology via collaboration. When we read what they said to each other, we understand what questions they had. As a result, their teacher provided wonderful scaffolding by participating in and observing their conversation. Keen observation of and involvement in children's uses of technology are very important for teachers and caregivers because they can offer appropriate and timely guidance when a "teachable moment" comes. The next step for these two boys could be to have an in-depth learning opportunity by creating an individual or small-group inquiry-based project related to their questions and obvious specific interest, such as trees and weather. In addition, the teacher can use technology (e.g., an iPad's digital camera to take some photos of trees, leaves, and weather changes, and a computer and a projector for presenting) for their project. It would enhance their curiosity and cohesive learning through real-life experiences and technology.

Derick. As noted earlier, children with attention issues and other types of learning difficulties often relate well to learning experiences that use step-by-step lessons, vivid colors and pictures, and many interactive responses

---

QUESTIONS FOR DISCUSSION

1. What should Nancy's parents be concerned about in using technology-augmented devices with their infant? Give some rules for its use for children under the age of 2.
2. When Jason and Edwin use technology for an in-depth project, how could you make the project more creative and meaningful? Is there any way you could promote their brain development more?
3. How should Mr. Santos monitor Derick's use of the technology-augmented learning devices to be sure that he is still gaining social skills and other experiences in addition to his excellent opportunities to learn on these devices?
4. What information or skills do you need to learn more about in order to support children's use of technology? Make a list by yourself or with colleagues or parents and discuss the list together. What different or similar learning needs do you all have? Consult with your director, principal, or early childhood education professionals about the list and then create a learning community for "Technology and Young Children." What decisions need to be made after this step? How can this become an ongoing exercise within your environment?
5. What online resources are helpful for supporting young children from diverse backgrounds? Create your own resource folder including the various sources you have found.

required by the child. Often technology-augmented devices can provide a structure that these students need. Derick has already shown that he attends to the iPad so many types of activities can be formatted for that device and for other such learning materials. It is important, however, that children such as Derick still have opportunities to interact with teachers and other children and to gradually extend their abilities through both human and technological interactions.

SUGGESTIONS FOR FURTHER READING

American Academy of Pediatrics Council on Communications and Media. (2016). Media and young minds. *Pediatrics, 138*(5), e2016–2591.

Bergen, D. (2000). Technology in the classroom: Linking technology and teaching practice. *Childhood Education, 76*(4), 252–253.

Burden, K., Kearney, M., & Hopkins, P. (2017). IPAC app evaluation rubric. Retreived from www.mobilelearningtoolkit.com/uploads/5/6/0/9/56096707/appevaluationinstrumentfinalrubric.pdf

DiCarlo, C. F., Schepis, M., & Flynn, L. (2009). Embedding sensory preferences in toys to enhance toy play in toddlers with disabilities. *Infants and Young Children, 22*(3), 187–199.

Lee, L. (2015). Young children, play, and technology: Meaningful ways of using technology and digital media. In D. P. Fromberg & D. Bergen (Eds.), *Play from Birth to Twelve: Contexts, Perspectives, and Meanings* (3rd ed., pp. 217–224). New York, NY: Routledge.

Melhuish, K., & Falloon, G. (2010). Looking to the future: M-learning with the iPad. Computers in New Zealand Schools: Learning, Leading, *Technology, 22*(3).

Tu, X., & Lee, L. (2019). Integrating digital media in early childhood education: A case study of using iPad in American Mid-Western preschools. *Journal of Studies in Chinese Early Childhood Education.* [Chinese], 54–59.

Walker, H. (2011). Evaluating the effectiveness of apps for mobile devices. *Journal of Special Education Technology, 26*(4), 59–63.

CHAPTER 7

Contemporary and Future Issues Related to Children's Brain Development

The authors of this book have suggested a range of ideas and teaching strategies for promoting children's healthy and positive brain development. Our goal has been to assist teachers, parents, and other caregivers in promoting that brain development. However, we also know that there are many contemporary and future societal actions that may have an impact on children's development and that these changing conditions may both enhance aspects of children's brain development and have negative influences on how children brains develop.

In this final chapter we discuss some issues that could have an impact on children's development in the future. First, we give a brief summary of the major factors that influence healthy brain development. Next, we discuss some of the issues related to the potential effects of contemporary environmental conditions on children's development. Then we review some predictions about how these changes in children's lives may change brain development in the future. Finally, we offer some suggestions for continuing to foster children's healthy brain development in changing society.

EMERGING ISSUES INFLUENCING ESSENTIAL CONDITIONS FOR HEALTHY BRAIN DEVELOPMENT

Essential conditions for healthy brain development have thus far remained accessible in every era of human existence. That is, while many young children throughout history and in various parts of the world may not have been in environments that promoted optimum brain development, there were no major differences in the access children had to the outdoors, to basic health and nourishment opportunities, and, especially, to time for play and physical interaction with the humans and environmental features of their worlds. The present, and especially future, eras in which humans will grow up seem likely to be somewhat different from those of the past because

technological advancements are changing the ways that infants and parents interact, the play experiences of young children, and the opportunities for time in natural world environments that were common child experiences in past centuries.

Because "everything is food" for the brain (Olds, 1998, p. 124), as types of human experiences change, human brains will develop differently, perhaps with the loss of some common skills and the addition of some skills that presently do not exist. It is especially likely that exposure of very young children to technology-augmented devices, which has begun to substitute for parent and/or teacher interpersonal interactions, as well as the loss of the children's active involvement in "natural world" experiences will have some significant effects on their brain development (Bergen, 2018). One example of a potential brain developmental change comes from the research on handwriting, which has been linked to brain development (James & Engelhardt, 2012). It is possible that the pervasive use of keyboard writing rather than handwriting may affect the development of portions of the brain that were involved in handwriting development (see Konnikova, 2014). It will be especially important to make these new experiences "additions" to children's lives rather having them result in the loss of traditional typical human and natural world experiences.

Emotional Development Issues

Some research is beginning to indicate that young children in contemporary society tend to have more negative emotional experiences and traumatic events than in previous generations (Cooper, Masi, & Vick, 2009). According to Gardner (1983), each person's emotional stability is critical in developing understanding of one's self and others in addition to general cognition and language (Gabbay, Oatis, Silva, & Hirsch, 2004).

In particular, toxic stress can significantly harm children's brain functions. Toxic stress, which can be caused by consistent poverty, malnutrition, child abuse, domestic violence, and parental mental problems, among other things, can interrupt children's academic performance, and even their physical and mental health into adulthood and throughout their lives (Odgers, 2015). It is important to understand that children may have ongoing problems in developing cognitive skills and emotional capacity to understand self and others, even when their negative environments are gone (Tronick, 2010; Tronick et al., 1978). As a result, dealing with young children's mental and emotional concerns as early as possible is extremely important. Of course, children can overcome adverse childhood experiences and problematic development can be improved. In some cases, children with varying degrees of toxic stress can resume their normal development. However, there is typically a longer adjustment period the older the child is at the onset of treatment and/or intervention (Romero-Martínez, Figueiredo, & Moya-Albiol, 2014). Also, in many cases reducing the stressors affecting children requires addressing the stresses on their families.

Lack of Social Interaction in School

Unfortunately, children's daily presence in the classroom is not a sufficient condition for the development of positive social skills (Laushey & Heflin, 2000). This may be because when children are in classrooms they spend "very little time being taught social skills (1 percent)" (La Paro, Rimm-Kauffman, & Pianta, 2006, p. 196). Kindergarten classrooms often provide a child's first experiences in learning to interact with peers and adults outside of their family and home contexts; therefore, they should offer children a safe space to practice new social emotional skills such as language use, conflict resolution, and friendship formation (Russell, Lee, Spieker, & Oxford, 2016). Despite research demonstrating the value of the relationship between education and social development in early childhood education, the social effects of school settings are often undermined or overlooked in favor of a more academic curriculum or schedule (Katz, 2015). The assumption is often that if the academic pieces are in place, the social components of effective education will naturally happen on their own.

In a study of social behavior in kindergarten, researchers measured the social behavior of 36 children enrolled in schools—private (n = 5) and public (n = 8)—across five learning contexts typically found in a kindergarten classroom: whole-group, small-group, free play, lunch, and recess (DiCarlo, Ota, & Deris, in press). Specifically, *prosocial behavior*—defined as a behavior that is helpful and demonstrated toward others—was measured across 3 years. This research indicates that prosocial behavior was virtually nonexistent across all five learning contexts across all 3 years. At the outset of this study, it seemed logical that one might find more social interaction in non-teacher-directed experiences, such as center time, lunch, or recess. Researchers found, however, that teachers often monitored the noise level of the classroom, which restricted social interaction, and seemed overly focused on progress on academic tasks, which rushed activities (e.g., lunch) that would seem to have allowed time for social interaction. At recess, observed teachers appeared to take a hands-off approach, and did not facilitate social games or any social interaction. If teachers do not have the time within the school day to address children's social interaction, when will this happen?

Parental Overuse of Technology

The behaviors of some parents also are of concern to those who want the best environments for young children's brain development. In today's world many adults use cellphones and other technology-augmented devices so often that they no longer have the "person-to-person" real interactions that adults typically have had with their children in past years. For example, some adults have been observed while with their children (even very young children) being completely engrossed in such devices at restaurants, in doctors' waiting rooms, at the park, and at other venues. Often the young children also have such devices, and there is little interpersonal interaction between parents and children.

This concept of "present absence," defined as the pervasive use of cellphones in social situations (Katz & Aakhus, 2002), can diminish the quality of the parent–child relationship (Kildare & Middlesmiss, 2017; Radesky et al., 2014). When participating in children's activities, it is important for parents to be present, both physically and mentally. Being distracted by a cellphone can cause parents and caregivers to be less sensitive and responsive to their child, and contribute to problem behaviors, as the child attempts to gain adults' attention (Kildare & Middlemiss, 2017). Also, overuse of cellphones can result in children who grow up to be more negative and less resilient (Myruski et al., 2017), children who feel unimportant (AVG Technologies, 2015), children whose social–emotional development can be stymied (UCI News, 2016), and children who exhibit feelings of sadness, anger, and loneliness (Steiner-Adair & Barker, 2013).

Research on parental use of technology dates back over 15 years and is compelling. Given the detrimental impact of cellphone usage when interacting with young children, research suggests that parents and caregivers limit their cellphone use when with children in order to promote healthy adult–child relationships.

Passive Rather Than Active Music Involvement

Historically, music activities and experiences for children were "active," meaning the child was involved in watching and hearing adults or other children make "live" music, or they were participating themselves. These activities included singing, drumming, clapping, and dancing. The earliest known musical instruments were "flutes" made from puncturing holes into bird bones dating back over 40,000 years (BBC News, 2012). Over time, more instruments were developed, and children were physically experiencing making music just as part of life by playing a simple instrument, dancing with an adult, or singing along with the family around a piano.

This active participation in making music as part of life allowed children to learn basic rhythm and pitch from "doing" music in a natural and comfortable setting. Even when recorded music came on the scene, much child participation in active music still took place. However, as more videos, computers, tablets, phones, video games, TVs, and recordings have come along, music experiences have become more passive. While technology tools can be beneficial in teaching music or assisting in learning, in general, a parent or teacher now must be far more intentional about creating a space for child participatory music making. Consequently, music experiences that involve parents and young children in group musical participation activities have become important (see Guilmartin & Levinowitz, 2003, 2009).

A study of music experiences in the homes of young children from seven different countries (Canada, Italy, Peru, Thailand, Turkey, UK, USA) found that in home settings digitized sounds were almost constantly present (Gillen, Cameron, Tapanya, Pinto, Hancock, Young, & Gamannossi, 2007). They came from many sources, including from toys with digitized songs, mobiles that played music, ringtones, and other sound-making devices in addition to TV, DVD, and other sources. Although some authors (e.g., Young, Street, & Davies; 2007) note that young children continue to contribute actively when engaged in these musical experiences, they also say that "new technologies and media resources are changing the nature of family musical practices and participation" (p. 97). It is easy to think that putting music "in front of a child or listening to music on a streaming platform is being "musical"; but when the active participatory component of music experience is missing, many opportunities for creating musical brain connections in early childhood are not happening, and this may be detrimental

to the child gaining the benefits of music learning. However, singing is using an "instrument" within our bodies that will not be affected by technology.

Decreasing Levels of Childhood Physical Activity

In part due to the influence of technology-augmented devices but also because of the present emphasis on rigid teaching standards in schools, adult-structured out-of-school learning experiences, and adult-directed sports activities, many of today's young children have little time for self-designed play and spontaneous learning activities. In contrast to the childhood experiences of children in past generations, in which adults remember many examples of child-controlled, extensive time periods of active play (see Davis & Bergen, 2014), today's children have many constraints that prevent them from engaging in long periods of active, self-directed, outdoor play, especially with groups of other children. In fact, outdoor play that is only lightly supervised by adults is almost nonexistent for today's children. In a recent report of the extent of physical activity observed in children throughout the world, the World Health Organization stated that childhood "inactivity" has become a "global threat" (see Gallagher, 2019). Because young children learn a great deal through their physical interactions and sensory experiences, this loss of active play—especially when chosen by the child—will certainly have an effect on their brain development processes.

RESILIENCE IN UNCERTAIN TIMES

The year 2020, with its COVID-19 pandemic, has reminded everyone that in order to survive and flourish, human beings often have to cope with world events requiring them to use their brains in ways that are creative, persistent, and courageous. Therefore, a major goal of those who care for and teach children must be to help their brains develop in ways that foster this human resilience. Resilience has been defined as "the process of, capacity for, or outcome of successful adaptation despite challenging or threatening circumstances" (Masten, Best, & Garmezy, 1990, p. 426). Alvord and Grados (2005, p. 238) state that resilience is composed of "those skills, attributes, and abilities that enable individuals to adapt to hardships, difficulties, and challenges." Some of the qualities of resilient humans that they identify are:

1. Proactive orientation (taking initiative and believing in one's own effectiveness)
2. Self-regulation (controlling one's attention, emotions, and behavior)
3. Connections/attachments (engaging in supportive parent/caregiver relationships)
4. Positive educational experiences (learning effectively, extending special talents)
5. Community support (participating in healthy, safe, encouraging wider environments)

Such qualities are fostered by adults who engage young children in positive, interesting, safe, and challenging experiences that promote their optimal brain development. The children who interact with such adults will thrive best in problematic and uncertain times. For specific suggestions for helping children in these times, see DiCarlo and Fazio-Brunson (2020).

THE ROLE OF EARLY CHILDHOOD PROFESSIONALS IN SUPPORTING CHILDREN'S BRAIN DEVELOPMENT

Because of these trends that are influencing the brain development of young children, the role of early childhood professionals has become even more important. They must be knowledgeable about how these early years provide the experiences that are essential for children's optimum development of neural connections, which are primarily obtained by their participation in active, physically involving, and creative experiences during these years. It is the hope of the authors that this book assists them in their creative work of children's brain building.

QUESTIONS FOR DISCUSSION

1. What are the most important behaviors that early childhood profession-als should model to promote young children's positive brain develop-ment in both their present and their future environments?
2. What types of professional development should be necessary for early childhood professionals to support young children's emotional, psy-chological, and mental well-being in our contemporary society?
3. How can early care environments help promote social interaction and physical activity for young children at school and how can we advocate for the importance of social interaction and physical activity when chil-dren are not in school?
4. With increasing technology and passive types of music learning and listening, what are some ways that teachers and parents can be musical with young children and model hands-on music-making experiences?

SUGGESTIONS FOR FURTHER READING

Bergen, D., Davis, D., & Abbitt, J. (2016). *Technology play and brain development: Infancy to adolescence and future implications.* New York, NY: Taylor & Francis.

Clark, S., & Lee, L. (2019). Technology enhanced classroom for low-income chil-dren's mathematical content learning: A case study. *International Journal of Information and Education Technology, 9*(1), 66–69.

DiCarlo, C. F., & Banajee, M. (2000). Using voice output devices to increase ini-tiations of young children with disabilities. *Journal of Early Intervention, 23*(3), 191–199.

References

AAP Council on Communications and Media (2016). Media and young minds. *Pediatrics* 138(5), e2016–2591.

Adibi, J. J., Marques, E. T., Jr., Cartus, A., & Beigi, R. H. (2016). Teratogenic effects of the Zika virus and the role of the placenta. *The Lancet*, *387*(10027), 1587–1590.

Agrawal, A., Scherrer, J. F., Grant, J. D., Sartor, C. E., Pergadia, M. L., Duncan, A. E . . . Xian, H. (2010). The effects of maternal smoking during pregnancy on offspring outcomes. *Preventive Medicine*, *50*(1–2), 13–18.

Alvord, M. K., & Grados, J. J. (2005). Enhancing resilience in children: A proactive approach. *Professional psychology: research and practice*, *36*(3), 238.

Ambady, N., & Bharucha, J. (2009). Culture and the brain. *Current Directions in Psychological Science*, *18*(6), 342–345.

American Academy of Pediatrics. (2018). Children and media tips from the American Academy of Pediatrics. Retrieved from https://www.aap.org/en-us/about-the-aap/ aap-press-room/news-features-and-safety-tips/Pages/Children-and-Media-Tips.asp

AVG Technologies (2015). Kids competing with mobile phones for parents' attention. Retrieved from https://now.avg.com/digital-diaries-kids-competing-with-mobile-phones-for-parents-attention

Bauer, P. J., Lukowski, A. F., & Pathman, T. (2011). Neuropsychology of middle childhood development (6 to 11 years old). In A. S. Davis (Ed.), *Handbook of pediatric neuropsychology* (p. 37–46). New York, NY: Springer.

BBC News (2012, May 25). Earliest music instruments found. Retrieved from www.bbc. com/news/science-environment-18196349

Bellini, S., & Akullian, J. (2007). A meta-analysis of video modeling and video self-modeling interventions for children and adolescents with autism spectrum disorders. *Exceptional children*, *73*(3), 264–287.

Bergen, D. (2018). Perspective: Potential effects of young children's virtual experiences on their brain development and other areas of development. *Early Childhood Psychology and Psychiatry*, *7*, 205–207.

Bergen, D., Reid, R., & Torelli, L. (2009). *Educating and caring for very young children: The infant/toddler curriculum* (2nd ed.). New York, NY: Teachers College Press.

Bergen, D., & Woodin, M . (2017). *Brain research and childhood education: Implications for educators, parents, and society*. New York, NY: Routledge.

Bielas, S., Higginbotham, H., Koizumi, H., Tanaka, T., & Gleeson, J. G. (2004). Cortical neuronal migration mutants suggest separate but intersecting pathways. *Annual Review of Cell and Developmental Biology*, *20*, 593–618.

Brown, T. T., & Jernigan, T. L. (2012). Brain development during the preschool years. *Neuropsychology Review*, *22*(4), 313–333.

Bruner, J. S. (1964). The course of cognitive growth. *American psychologist*, *19*(1), 1.

Burden, K. J., & Kearney, M. (2017). Investigating and critiquing teacher educators' mobile learning practices. *Interactive Technology and Smart Education*.

Chua, A., Prat, I., Nuebling, C. M., Wood, D., & Moussy, F. (2017). Update on Zika diagnostic tests and WHO's related activities. *PLOS Neglected Tropical Diseases, 11*(2), doi.org/10.1371/journal.pntd.0005269.

Chugani, H. T. (1999). PET scanning studies of human brain development and plasticity. *Developmental Neuropsychology, 16*(3), 379–381.

Cooper, J. L., Masi, R., & Vick, J. (2009). *Social–emotional development in early childhood: What every policymaker should know.* New York, NY: National Center for Children in Poverty.

Corn, H. J. M., & Bishop, D. I. (2010). Intrauterine development of the central nervous system. In A. S. Davis (Ed.), *Handbook of pediatric neuropsychology* (pp. 1–14). New York: Springer.

Coudé, G., Festante, F., Cilia, A., Loiacono, V., Bimbi, M., Fogassi, L., & Ferrari, P. F. (2016). Mirror neurons of ventral premotor cortex are modulated by social cues provided by others' gaze. *Journal of Neuroscience, 36*(11), 3145–3156.

Davis, D., & Bergen, D. (2014). Relationships among play behaviors reported by college students and their responses to moral issues: A pilot study. *Journal of Research in Childhood Education, 28,* 484–498.

DiCarlo, C. F., & Banajee, M. (2000). Using voice output devices to increase initiations of young children with disabilities. *Journal of Early Intervention, 23*(3), 191–199. Retrieved from jei.sagepub.com/content/23/3/191.full.pdf+html

DiCarlo, C. F., & Fazio-Brunson, M. (2020, September/October). Navigating quarantine with young children. *Exchange,* 40–42.

DiCarlo, C. F., Ota, C. & Deris, A. (in press). An ecobehavioral analysis of social behavior across learning contexts in kindergarten. *Early Childhood Education Journal.*

DiCarlo, C. F., Schepis, M. M., & Flynn, L. (2009). Embedding sensory preference into toys to enhance toy play in toddlers with disabilities. *Infants & Young Children, 22*(3), 188–200.

DiCarlo, C. F., Stricklin, S., Banajee, M., & Reid, D. (2001). Effects of manual signing on communicative vocalizations by toddlers with and without disabilities in inclusive classrooms. *The Journal of the Association for Persons with Severe Handicaps, 26*(2), 1–7.

Domènech Rodriguez, M. M., Donovick, M. R., & Crowley, S. L. (2009). Parenting styles in a cultural context: Observations of "protective parenting" in first-generation Latinos. *Family Process, 48*(2), 195–210.

Edwards, C., Gandini, L., & Forman, G. (Eds.). (1998). *The hundred languages of children: The reggio emilia approach [to early childhood education]-advanced reflections.* Ablex.

Eliot, L. (1999) *What's going on in there? How the brain and mind develop in the first five-years of life.* New York, NY: Bantam Books.

Gabbay, V., Oatis, M. D., Silva, R. R., & Hirsch, G. (2004). Epidemiological aspects of PTSD in children and adolescents. In R. R. Silva (Ed.), *Posttraumatic stress disorders in children and adolescents: Handbook* (pp. 1–17). New York, NY: Norton.

Gallagher, J. (2019, November 22). "Global epidemic" of childhood inactivity. In BBC News [Website]. Retrieved from www.bbc.com/news/health-50466061

Gardner, H. (1983). *The theory of multiple intelligences.* New York, NY: Heinemann.

Gillen, J., Cameron, C. A., Tapanya, S., Pinto, G., Hancock, R., Young, S., Gamannossi, B. A. (2007). A day in the life: Advancing a methodology for the cultural study of development and learning in early childhood. *Early Child Development and Care, 177*(2), 207–218.

Graven, S. N., & Browne, J. V. (2008). Auditory development in the fetus and infant. *Newborn and Infant Nursing Reviews, 8*(4), 187–193.

Guilmartin, K. K., & Levinowitz, L. M. (2003). *Music and your child: A guide for parents and caregivers.* Princeton, NJ: Music Together.

Guilmartin, K. K., & Levinowitz, L. M. (2009). *Music Together family favorites songbook for teachers.* Princeton, NJ: Music Together.

Hart, B., & Risley, T. R. (1974). Using preschool materials to modify the language of disadvantaged children. *Journal of Applied Behavior Analysis, 7*(2), 243–256. Retrieved from www.ncbi.nlm.nih.gov/pmc/articles/PMC1311963/pdf/jaba00060-0073.pdf

Hart, B., & Risley, T. R. (1975). Incidental teaching of language in the preschool. *Journal of Applied Behavior Analysis, 8*(4), 411–420.

Hepper, P. G., & Shahidullah, B. S. (1994). The development of fetal hearing. *Fetal and Maternal Medicine Review, 6*(3), 167–179.

Hillman, M., & Marshall, J. (2009). Evaluation of digital media for emergent literacy. *Computers in the Schools, 26*(4), 256–270

Honein, M. A., Paulozzi, L. J., & Watkins, M. L. (2001). Maternal smoking and birth defects: validity of birth certificate data for effect estimation. *Public Health Reports, 116*(4), 327.

James, K. H., & Engelhardt, L. (2012). The effects of handwriting experience on functional brain development in pre-literate children. *Trends in Neuroscience and Education, 1*(1), 32–42. https://doi.org/10.1016/j.tine.2012.08.001

Katz, J. (2015). Implementing the Three Block Model of Universal Design for Learning: Effects on teachers' self-efficacy, stress, and job satisfaction in inclusive classrooms K–12. *International Journal of Inclusive Education, 19*(1), 1–20.

Katz, J. E., & Aakhus, M. (Eds.). (2002). *Perpetual contact: Mobile communication, private talk, public performance.* New York, NY: Cambridge University Press.

Kildare, C. A., & Middlemiss, W. (2017). Impact of parents mobile device use on parent-child interaction: A literature review. *Computers in Human Behavior, 75,* 579–593.

Konnikova, M. (2014, June 2). What's lost as handwriting fades. *The New York Times,* 2. Retrieved from www.nytimes.com/2014/06/03/science/whats-lost-as-handwriting-fades.html.

La Paro, K. M., Rimm-Kaufman, S. E., & Pianta, R. C. (2006). Kindergarten to 1st grade: Classroom characteristics and the stability and change of children's classroom experiences. *Journal of Research in Childhood Education, 21*(2), 189–202.

Laushey, K. M., & Heflin, L. J. (2000). Enhancing social skills of kindergarten children with autism through the training of multiple peers as tutors. *Journal of autism and developmental disorders, 30*(3), 183–193.

Lee, L. (2019). When technology met real-life experiences: Science curriculum project with technology for low-income Latino preschoolers. In N. Kucirkova, J. Rowsell, & G. Falloon (Eds.). *The Routledge international handbook of learning with technology in early childhood* (pp. 338–348). New York, NY: Routledge.

Liu, D., Sabbagh, M. A., Gehring, W. J., & Wellman, H. M. (2009). Neural correlates of children's theory of mind development. *Child development, 80*(2), 318–326.

Maitre, N. L., Key, A. P., Chorna, O. D., Slaughters, J. C., Matusz, P. J., Wallace, M. T., & Murray, M. M. (2017). The dual nature of early-life experience on somatosensory processing in the human infant brain. *Current Biology, 27*(7), 1048–1054. doi:10.1016/j.cub.2017.02.036

Masten, A. S., Best, K. M., & Garmezy, N. (1990). Resilience and development: Contributions from the study of children who overcome adversity. *Development and Psychopathology, 2,* 425–444.

Melhuish, K., & Falloon, G. (2010). Looking to the future: M-learning with the iPad. *Computers in New Zealand Schools: Learning, Leading, Technology, 22*(3). Retrieved from https://www.researchgate.net/publication/261438525_Looking_to_the_Future_M-Learning_with_the_iPad

Mischel, W. (2015). *The marshmallow test: Why self-control is the engine of success.* New York, NY: Little, Brown.

Myruski, S., Bonanno, G. A., Gulyayeva, O., Egan, L. J., & Dennis-Tiwary, T. A. (2017).

Neurocognitive assessment of emotional context sensitivity. *Cognitive, Affective, & Behavioral Neuroscience, 17*(5), 1058–1071.

National Association for the Education of Young Children (NAEYC) & Fred Rogers Center for Early Learning and Children's Media at Saint Vincent College (2012). *Technology and interactive media as tools in early childhood programs serving children from birth through age 8* [Position statement]. Washington, DC: NAEYC.

Neville, H., Andersson, A., Bagdade, O., Bell, T., Currin, J., Fanning, J., . . . & Paulsen, D. (2008). Effects of music training on brain and cognitive development in under-privileged 3- to 5-year-old children: Preliminary results. In M. Gazzaniga, C, Absury, & B. Rich (Eds.), *Learning, arts, and the brain: The Dana Consortium report on arts and cognition* (pp. 105–106). New York, NY: Dana Foundation.

Odgers, C. L. (2015). Income inequality and the developing child: Is it all relative? *American Psychologist, 70*(8), 722.

Ojala, M. (2000) Parent and teacher expectations for developing young children: A cross-cultural comparison between Ireland and Finland. *European Early Childhood Education Research Journal, 8*(2), 39–61.

Olds, A. R. (1998). Places of beauty. In D. Bergen (Ed.). *Readings from play as a medium for learning and development* (pp. 123–127). Olney, MD: Association for Childhood Education International.

Perry, B. D. (1996). Incubated in terror: Neurodevelopmental factors in the "cycle of violence." In J. D. Osofsky (Ed.), *Children, youth, and violence: Searching for solutions* (pp. 124–148). New York, NY: Guilford Press.

Piaget, J. (1952). *The origins of intelligence.* New York, NY: Free Press.

Piazza, E., Lasenfratz, L, Hasson, U., & Lew-Williams, C. (2020). Infant and adult brains are coupled to the dynamics of natural communication. *Psychological Science, 31*(1) 6–17. doi:10.1177/0956797619878698

Pugh, K. R., Landi, N., Preston, J. L., Mencl, W. E., Austin, A. C., Sibley, D., . . . Frost, S. J. (2013). The relationship between phonological and auditory processing and brain organization in beginning readers. *Brain and Language, 125*(2), 173–183. Retrieved from www.ncbi.nlm.nih.gov/pmc/articles/PMC3417084/

Radesky, J. S., Kistin, C. J., Zuckerman, B., Nitzberg, K., Gross, J., Kaplan-Sanoff, M., . . . & Silverstein, M. (2014). Patterns of mobile device use by caregivers and children during meals in fast food restaurants. *Pediatrics, 133*(4), e843–e849.

Rideout, V. J., & Hamel, E. (2006). *The media family: Electronic media in the lives of infants, toddlers, preschoolers and their parents.* Henry J. Kaiser Family Foundation.

Rizzolatti, G., & Craighero, L. (2004). The mirror-neuron system. *Annual Review of Neuroscience, 27*, 169–192.

Robb, M., Catalano, R., Smith, T., Polojac, S., Figlar, M., Minzenberg, B., & Schomburg, R. (2013). *Checklist for identifying exemplary uses of technology and interactive media for early learning: The Pennsylvania digital media literacy project.* Latrobe, PA: Fred Rogers Center for Early Learning and Children's Media at Saint Vincent College.

Roberts, G., Quach, J., Mensah, F., Gathercole, S., Gold, L., Anderson, P., . . . & Wake, M. (2015). Schooling duration rather than chronological age predicts working memory between 6 and 7 years: Memory Maestros study. *Journal of Developmental & Behavioral Pediatrics, 36*(2), 68–74.

Romero-Martínez, A., Figueiredo, B., & Moya-Albiol, L. (2014). Childhood history of abuse and child abuse potential: The role of parent's gender and timing of childhood abuse. *Child abuse & neglect, 38*(3), 510–516.

Russell, B. S., Lee, J. O., Spieker, S., & Oxford, M. L. (2016). Parenting and preschool self-regulation as predictors of social emotional competence in 1st grade. *Journal of Research in Childhood Education, 30*(2), 153–169.

Sangal, R. B., & Sangal, J. M. (1996). Topography of auditory and visual P300 in normal children. *Clinical Electroencephalography, 27*(1), 46–51.

Schore, A. N. (2001). Effects of a secure attachment relationship on right brain development, affect regulation, and infant mental health. *Infant Mental Health Journal*, 22(1–2), 7–66.

Schulkind, L. M. (2015). Teaching Music to Gifted Children. In *Applied Practice for Educators of Gifted and Able Learners* (pp. 441–453). SensePublishers, Rotterdam.

Siegel, D. J. (2015). *The developing mind: How relationships and the brain interact to shape who we are*. New York, NY: Guilford Press.

Steiner-Adair, C., & Barker, T. H. (2013). *The big disconnect: Protecting childhood and family relationships in the digital age*. New York, NY: Harper Business.

Sun, H. (2017, April). Study on Orff's music teaching method. In 2017 International Conference on Innovations in Economic Management and Social Science (IEMSS 2017). https://doi.org/10.2991/iemss-17.2017.251

Tomasello, M., & Carpenter, M. (2007). Shared intentionality. *Developmental science*, 10(1), 121–125.

Trainor, L. J., Marie, C., Gerry, D., Whiskin, E., & Unrau, A. (2012). Becoming musically enculturated: Effects of music classes for infants on brain and behavior. *Annals of the New York Academy of Sciences*, 1252(1), 129–138.

Tronick, E., Als, H., Adamson, L., Wise, S., & Brazelton, T.B. (1978). The infant's response to entrapment between contradictory messages in face-to-face interaction. *Journal of the American Academy of Child Psychiatry*, 17(1), 1–13.

Tronick, E. Z. (2010). Infants and mothers: Self- and mutual regulation and meaning making. In B. M. Lester & J. D. Sparrow (Eds.), *Nurturing children and families: Building on the legacy of T. Berry Brazelton* (pp. 83–94). Malden, MA: Wiley-Blackwell

UCI News (January 6, 2015). Put the cellphone away! Fragmented baby care can affect brain development: UCI study shows maternal infant-rearing link to adolescent depression. Retrieved from https://news.uci.edu/2016/01/05/put-the-cellphone-away-fragmented-baby-care-can-affect-brain-development/

Varela, R. E., Vernberg, E. M., Sanchez-Sosa, J. J., Riveros, A., Mitchell, M., & Mashunkashey, J. (2004). Parenting style of Mexican, Mexican American, and Caucasian–non-Hispanic families: Social context and cultural influences. *Journal of Family Psychology*, 18(4), 651–657.

Vygotsky, L. S. (1978). *Mind in society: The development of higher psychological processes* (M. Cole, V. John-Steiner, S. Scribner, & E. Souberman, Eds.). Cambridge, MA: Harvard University Press.

Walker, L. (2011). My teacher is an Android: Engaging learners through an Android application. *Changing Demands, Changing Directions. Proceedings ASCILITE Hobart*, 1270–1274.

Warschauer, M., Knobel, M., & Stone, L. (2004). Technology and equity in schooling: Deconstructing the digital divide. *Educational policy*, 18(4), 562–588.

Young, S., Street, A., & Davies, E. (2007). The Music One-to-One project: Developing approaches to music with parents and under-two-year-olds. *European Early Childhood Education Research Journal*, 15(2), 253–267.

Index

About the Authors

Doris Bergen is a Distinguished Professor of Educational Psychology Emerita at Miami University in Oxford, Ohio. Before her university career began, she taught preschool and 2nd grade. At the university she taught courses on child development, early childhood curriculum, play and humor development, and brain development. Her research has included the study of play and humor development, effects of technology-enhanced toys on play, adult memories of childhood play, and development of gifted children's humor. She is a Miami University Distinguished Scholar, having published numerous books and articles on these topics. She also is a past president of the National Association of Early Childhood Teacher Educators.

Lena Lee is a Professor of Teacher Education at Miami University in Oxford, Ohio. In 2011 she received the American Educational Research Association (AERA) Emerging Scholar Award from the Critical Perspective of Early Childhood Education SIG. She also has written numerous book chapters and journal article publications related to the effects of technology on children's learning and development. She was the principle investigator on a 6–year enrichment grant for low-income preschool children, which involved university students in early childhood education participating with children in local preschools.

Cynthia DiCarlo is Professor of Education at Louisiana State University and is also the Executive Director of the Early Childhood Education Laboratory Preschool. She is certified in both birth to kindergarten and early intervention and has worked with children, birth to age 5, in public and private settings in center, community childcare, and home-based settings. At LSU, she holds the W. H. LeBlanc LSU Alumni Association Departmental Endowed Professorship. She has published over 50 refereed articles on early childhood, and her research on children's attention during whole-group instruction received the 2012 Research Paper of the Year from the *Journal of Research in Childhood Education.*

Gail Burnett is the owner of Miss Gail Music. She received a Teachers' Choice Award for exceptional quality Preschool Curriculum and a Parents' Choice Award for the music she has created for young children. In addition to teaching parent/child classes that focus on helping children make brain connections for music and other types of early learning, she has developed a program to educate early childhood teachers on how to implement music effectively in the classroom. She performs interactive movement shows for schools, events, parties, and children's venues. She has presented at many national early childhood conferences. She is also a professional cellist.